Coach for Christ

Coach for Christ

We Are All Coaches

Mike Roman IV

RESOURCE *Publications* · Eugene, Oregon

COACH FOR CHRIST
We Are All Coaches

Resource Publications
An Imprint of Wipf and Stock Publishers
199 W. 8th Ave., Suite 3
Eugene, OR 97401

www.wipfandstock.com

PAPERBACK ISBN: 978-1-6667-6400-0
HARDCOVER ISBN: 978-1-6667-6401-7
EBOOK ISBN: 978-1-6667-6402-4

VERSION NUMBER 050823

For the Man that will stand from the beginning to the end. For my mom Kerri, my dad Mike, and my sister Chelsea.

Contents

Scripture Abbreviations

OT

Genesis—Gen
Exodus—Exod
Leviticus—Lev
Numbers—Num
Deuteronomy—Deut
Joshua—Josh
Judges—Judg
Ruth—Ruth
1 Samuel—1 Sam
2 Samuel—2 Sam
1 Kings—1 Kgs
2 Kings—2 Kgs
1 Chronicles—1 Chr
2 Chronicles—2 Chr
Ezra—Ezra
Nehemiah—Neh
Esther—Esth
Job—Job
Psalms—Ps (Pss when citing multiple chapters at once)
Proverbs—Prov
Ecclesiastes (or Qoheleth)—Eccl (or Qoh)
Song of Solomon—Song
Isaiah—Isa
Jeremiah—Jer
Lamentations—Lam
Ezekiel—Ezek
Daniel—Dan
Hosea—Hos
Joel—Joel
Amos—Amos
Obadiah—Obad
Jonah—Jon
Micah—Mic
Nahum—Nah
Habakkuk—Hab
Zephaniah—Zeph
Haggai—Hag
Zechariah—Zech
Malachi—Mal

NT

Matthew—Matt
Mark—Mark
Luke—Luke
John—John
Acts—Acts
Romans—Rom
1 Corinthians—1 Cor
2 Corinthians—2 Cor
Galatians—Gal
Ephesians—Eph

Philippians—Phil

Colossians—Col

1 Thessalonians—1 Thess

2 Thessalonians—2 Thess

1 Timothy—1 Tim

2 Timothy—2 Tim

Titus—Titus

Philemon—Phlm

Hebrews—Heb

James—Jas

1 Peter—1 Pet

2 Peter—2 Pet

1 John—1 John

2 John—2 John

3 John—3 John

Jude—Jude

Revelation—Rev

Before you begin to read *Coach for Christ*, I want to mention one important point. Throughout the chapters of this book, you will notice many super-scripts after certain sentences. These superscripts directly reference the Scriptures. If you choose, you may follow along with your Bible and flip to the "Notes" section in the back of the book when you see a superscript so you will know exactly where to find these verses. By doing this, I hope it will help build your faith and knowledge of our Lord, Redeemer, and Savior, as it certainly has mine. (Please note that the ESV of the Bible is used unless otherwise specified in the "Notes" section.)

We are all coaches and we all have someone who we can influence in a positive way. As children of God, we are called to emulate the greatest coach this world has ever known, Jesus Christ. It is my hope that through this book, you are able to see how great our God is and the impact he can have on us if we let him.

I hope you enjoy the message.

Part I—The Journey

BEFORE I START THE journey of *Coach for Christ*, I need to thank the One who put it in my heart to write this book, Jesus. He has given me a Passion that I will never let go, and I hope by writing this book, you can further walk with him in your daily life as a coach. I want this book to reach a very broad audience and I will attempt to do so by expanding the definition of "coach." Whether you are a parent, a school teacher, a husband, a sibling, a friend, a sports coach, or a strength and conditioning coach, we are all coaches. We all have influence on someone and we all need guidance. Having a mentor or companion is something that we all need as humans. It is something that God has put within us and it has been that way since the beginning. That is clear when God wanted to give Adam a helper fit for him, Eve. All students need that teacher to look up to, all siblings need that big brother or sister to depend on, and all athletes need that coach that they can count on and trust with anything. And with every coach, there are morals, principles, and standards that he or she should live by in order to consistently influence others in a positive way. It is with this book that I hope to present the principles of the greatest mentor and coach that this world has ever known, Jesus Christ. I hope that you are able to utilize these principles throughout your daily walk with Jesus to not only improve your relationship with him every day, but to influence others in hopes of them seeing Christ through you.

I first want to describe myself and my continuing journey as a Christian so you understand who I am as a coach and what I set my identity in. By doing so, I hope you will be able to apply his teachings to your life and to who you are as a coach. But before I do, I must state that I am by no means an expert on the teachings of Jesus nor am I claiming to be. I am not perfect nor will I ever come close to being perfect. I am a sinner like the rest of us and I am always looking for the bread that Christ provides. The teachings and principles that I will talk about are by no means all of them.

The principles that I will talk about throughout this book are the ones that help me live to the fullest with Jesus every day. I hope that this book opens people's eyes to the one who brings true satisfaction and wisdom. As previously stated, we all need guidance and comfort. Every coach also needs someone they can look to for advice. There is no better coach and mentor to look up to than Jesus. He is the way to being the best coach you can be in life because he provides an answer to every question. He is the one who is willing to be your rock if you allow him to set your foundation. Throughout all the teachings he provides, I believe they can be centered upon two sacred words that he spoke multiple times, "Follow Me." By setting our foundation in him and following what he wants us to become through him, we can influence people in ways that God in the flesh intended us to. This is clear to us when he stated after his resurrection, "Go therefore and make disciples of all nations."[1] It is my hope that I can effectively articulate the teachings of Christ to you that have the most profound impact on my life not only as a coach, but as a man of Jesus Christ. Again, I am not a theologian and I am not claiming to have expertise on the teachings and history of Jesus. But what I do have is passion. I have a burning desire to live for Jesus every day and even though I fall short, I try to give everything I have for him as a man of faith. I know the fire he has put in my heart has always been lit, but that fire has grown bigger and hotter ever since he opened the door to how he wants me to serve him, and that is by being a coach to others. I would now like to backtrack and further explain how that door was opened and what my role as a coach is.

1—The Beginning of a Journey

AS A YOUNG BOY growing up in Stuart, Florida, I regularly attended church with my parents and sister. I always knew who Jesus was, and I always knew that he was my big brother, my defender, my counselor, and my comforter. I knew that I could always run to him in the best of times and when times seemed bleak. But in my late high school years, I deeply longed for a greater relationship with Jesus. I not only wanted more of him, but I wanted him to give me something in my life that I had a passion for. Something in my life that I could wake up for every day and truly enjoy what I do. With his guidance, I wanted to find something that we could pursue together. As time progresses, it is obvious that he heard me because his journey for us becomes clearer and clearer every day. With that being said, I believe that journey started when I got rejected by the college I wanted to go to most.

As previously mentioned, I grew up in Stuart, Florida as a young boy. When I was about ten years old, my family moved to Indianapolis, Indiana and we were only about fifteen minutes from the downtown area. Fortunately for our family, this was the time when Peyton Manning was throwing absolute dimes to guys like Marvin Harrison, Reggie Wayne, Dallas Clark, and Brandon Stokley. My family and I watched a lot of Indianapolis Colts football and we were lucky enough to see some big games! Not only did we see a lot of them on TV, but my parents surprised me with tickets sometimes as well! This was a huge gesture from my parents but it does not compare to how selfless, caring, loving, and compassionate they are. My mom and dad mean the world to me and I would not be the man I am today without them. They have helped my sister and I through thick and thin and have always been on our side, even when we are wrong. They've wanted the best for us ever since we were born. An example of this was when they opened a college fund for us as children when we were growing up in Florida. My sister and I were fortunate enough to go back to the state where we grew up as young children for college.

My sister, Chelsea, was a senior in high school when I was a freshman. She was the president of student council and she also ran cross country and track. To say the least, I had great company to look up to and I wanted to attempt to follow in her footsteps as my high school years progressed. It wasn't my interest to be student council president but I still wanted to be successful like she was. As her high school years were coming to a close, she decided to attend the University of Central Florida starting in the summer of 2009. The Roman family all packed as a team to make the move easy for her. As we approached Orlando, I was so pumped. I was thinking to myself, "Holy smokes, people actually get to go to college around here?" There are so many fun things to do in Orlando, you would have to try really hard to not find something to do. You could choose from the multiple amusement parks they have, you could go dancing or go out to eat at practically any restaurant under the sun, or you could hit up a UCF sporting event. On top of all the fun you could have, the campus is absolutely beautiful and the infrastructure is incredible. When we first visited UCF, there was no doubt in my mind that this was where I wanted to go. My sister graduated as student council president and she was going to a great university back in Florida. I wanted to follow in her footsteps so bad and I was sure I would be coming here after I graduated high school.

However, at the time, I had no idea what I wanted to do with my life from a vocational standpoint. All I knew is that I wanted to be a UCF Knight. This desire only increased when we went to visit my sister during homecoming that fall. That weekend consisted of fun times with the whole family and some beautiful weather. To top it off, we went to the football game and it had the most electric atmosphere that I have ever been a part of. Imagine yourself being in a student section that gets absolutely rowdy as they scream "UCF KNIGHTS" during a remix of "Seven Nation Army." That moment sealed the deal for me. I wanted to be a part of this atmosphere and I wanted to be a Knight. My family and I thanked Chelsea for an awesome weekend and I left daydreaming and imagining myself at this school in the coming years. I was hoping that I could start at UCF as soon as possible, but unfortunately, I still had three years of high school to finish before I could make my way down here.

The next few years of high school were great for me. I was able to make a lot of awesome friends who I still keep in touch with today. We went to football or basketball games on Friday nights, played backyard football on a regular basis, or just hung out after school to finish homework. I did have a ton of fun with my buddies during my first two years of high school, but I was still laser-focused. I concentrated on getting great grades, I stayed involved in extracurricular activities, and I made sure I always had a good rapport with my teachers. I still had my eye on the prize and that was getting into UCF. Near the end of my sophomore year, I maintained close to a 3.8 GPA while being a member of student council and playing on the school's tennis and baseball teams. I knew if I kept this up, there was no doubt in my mind that I would get into the school of my dreams. I knew that Chelsea already attending UCF would give me a huge advantage in the application process as well.

As my junior year approached, I maintained my laser focus and I wanted to make sure that I gave everything I had in every class I took, or every group I wanted to associate myself with, like Relay for Life. I didn't want any grade or lack of ineffectiveness in my résumé to be the reason I didn't get accepted. I tried my hardest to keep all my grades as As and Bs while keeping my extracurricular activities and volunteer hours up.

But as I previously mentioned, during my late high school years I needed God. I desperately longed to have an intimate relationship with Jesus. I know the previous page has just gone over my small journey of high school, but I do not want you to pass over those last two sentences like they are similar to the rest. Words on a page obviously can't describe when someone greatly burns in their heart for a relationship with Jesus. And when I say I needed God, I mean it with everything I have. Anyone who truly knows Jesus can agree wholeheartedly that "The Lord is near to the brokenhearted and saves the crushed in spirit."[2] When I say I have been on my knees before and cried to God, I have been there. When I say I have cried to God in such a way that has changed my life forever, I have been there. Please do not think that I cried to God asking him to allow me to get into UCF. My plea and cry to him had nothing to do with college. But it did have everything to do with my desire for him to open my eyes and ears so I could understand him more with my heart.[3]

2—Jesus, the True Champion

AT THE BEGINNING OF this book, I stated that Jesus has given me a Passion that I will never let go. Also, when I say the word, Passion, I don't relate it to its typical definition of having a very strong desire and love to do something. Passion has a very deep meaning for me. Now please don't get me wrong, when someone says they are passionate about something, I think it is awesome. For example, if someone tells me, "Mike, I am so passionate about basketball! I can play all day!" Or, "Mike, the passion I have for reading is so great! I could keep my head in a book all day long!" I think it is so awesome when people have found something that they truly love. By no means do I think I am better than anyone else. But I want to express to you my meaning of the word "Passion." As said before, words on a page cannot come close to truly expressing a relationship with Christ, but as you read the rest of this book, I hope you can internally understand how I feel about Jesus and the burning Passion I have for him as well as hoping you have the same for him too.

Now the definition I compare the word "Passion" with is not new. It is actually in the Merriam-Webster dictionary (which fires me up!). Passion to me and according to the Merriam-Webster dictionary is the sufferings of Christ between the Last Supper and his death.[4] When I use the word "Passion," this is what I relate it to. Any time I say I am Passionate about something, I relate it to the passion of the Christ. Personally, I don't think humans can comprehend what passion is unless it is done through Jesus. Jesus went through the inhumane process of verberatio within his passion, which is the scourging and flogging of someone with a tool called a flagellum. The flagellum that the Romans used on Jesus was not a standard whip that would just leave severe bruises and agonizing wounds. This torturous instrument was about three feet long and its ends were weighted with lead balls and pieces of bone. Jesus was bound to a frame, stripped,

6

and lacerated with this instrument until practically the point of death. The Romans delivered these lacerations with zero consideration for his health, and this left Jesus in a state that I could not even fathom. According to the church historian Eusebius of Caesarea in his book *Ecclesiastical History*, he verifies these horrible events by stating, "They say that the bystanders were struck with amazement when they saw them lacerated with scourges even to the innermost veins and arteries, so that the hidden inward parts of the body, both their bowels and their members, were exposed to view."[5]

Jesus was not supposed to be crucified after this process until the Jews pleaded to Pontius Pilate to have a murderer released and have Jesus crucified. Pilate gave them their desire, having said, "I am innocent of this man's blood; see it to yourselves,"[6] as he washed his hands in a bowl of water. Shortly after the agonizing and unfathomable pain he must have gone through by standing in front of these people while they pleaded for his crucifixion, Jesus then had a crown of thorns driven into his head while being mocked and spit on before he had to carry his cross to his crucifixion site at Golgotha (which means "Place of the Skull"). The Champion that this Man is then embraced his cross and put it on his back (weighing hundreds of pounds) to carry it through the "way of suffering" (the path Jesus followed to Golgotha).

During Jesus's passion, he continued to be whipped and beaten on his way to Golgotha while carrying his cross. "As they went out, they found a man of Cyrene, Simon by name. They compelled this man to carry his cross."[7] Jesus at this moment needed help. I want to go on a short tangent by saying that in hard times, we all need someone. We all need that mentor in tough times, and we all need that coach to depend on. Could Jesus, God in the flesh, have easily taken that cross and popped it over his head to his destination? Absolutely. But we know that God so loved the world that he gave his only Son.[8] He so loved us as people, that he needed to clearly show us the Way, the Truth, and the Life[9] (which was him). He cared for us so much, that he "emptied himself, by taking the form of a servant, being born in the likeness of men. And being found in human form, he humbled himself by becoming obedient to the point of death, even death on a cross."[10] Jesus did not have to come into the world to save us as sinners. He came into the world because he wants us dearly, more than we could ever imagine as humans. He wants to be our best friend, our defender, and our personal coach. He has been there since the beginning, and will be there until the end.

Jesus has always been there. This is clear in the very first chapter of Genesis. In the beginning, on the first day of existence, God said, "Let there be light," and there was light.[11] "And God saw that the light was good."[12] I know that some people might have just read that verse and raised their eyebrows. But as you read through the first chapter of Genesis, you will see that on the fourth day, God created the two great lights—"the greater light to rule the day and the lesser light to rule the night—and the stars."[13] Wouldn't you find it strange that God made light before the sun, moon, and stars? I sure would. However, it is clear that Jesus was, is, and will always be the light. In the book of John, Jesus states, "I am the light of the world. Whoever follows me will not walk in darkness, but will have the light of life."[14] Jesus was having a discussion with the Pharisees (a religious group that was obsessive about Jewish law and constantly ridiculed and disliked Jesus) when he stated this. Jesus went on to say, "Even if I do bear witness about myself, my testimony is true, for I know where I came from and where I am going."[15] Jesus is the Light, the Way, the Truth, and the Life and was with the Father since the very beginning.

Knowing this, we need to understand that he was and always will be. God informed Moses at Horeb, the mountain of God, that he wanted him to free his people, the children of Israel, out of Egypt. Here, God revealed himself in a flame of fire out of the midst of a bush. Moses looked, and saw the bush was burning, but it was not consumed.[16] In awe, Moses said to God, "If I come to the people of Israel and say to them, 'The God of your fathers has sent me to you,' and they ask me, 'What is his name?' what shall I say to them?" And God said to Moses, "I AM WHO I AM." And he said, "Say this to the people of Israel, 'I AM has sent me to you.'"[17]

While Jesus was being questioned by the Jews in the temple in John 8, he goes onto teach that "if anyone keeps my word, he will never see death."[18] To say the least, the Jews did not like this. They ridiculed him and profoundly stated to him, "Are you greater than our father Abraham, who died? And the prophets died! Who do you make yourself out to be?"[19] Jesus responds by saying, "Your father Abraham rejoiced that he would see my day. He saw it and was glad. So the Jews said to him, 'You are not yet fifty years old, and have you seen Abraham?' Jesus said to them, 'Truly, truly, I say to you, before Abraham was, I am.'"[20] God stated to Moses in the burning bush, "I AM." And Jesus said to the Jews, "I AM." Jesus was, is, and will always be. Our God is three in one.

After his resurrection, when Jesus appeared to John on the island of Patmos in the book of Revelation, he profoundly stated, "Behold, I am coming soon, bringing my recompense with me, to repay each one for what he has done. I am the Alpha and the Omega, the first and the last, the beginning and the end."[21] He is the root and the descendant of David, the bright morning star.[22] Jesus, fulfilling every prophecy within the Old Testament, made a new covenant with us as people, putting his law within us, desiring to write it on our hearts.[23]

Our God came to earth in the flesh not to abolish Jewish law, but to fulfill it and set a new standard for us. This standard is having faith through Jesus and accepting his grace so we are able to be right with God. We need his grace because no matter how hard we try, we all sin and fall short of God's perfection. This is why Jesus came. He is three in one that physically showed us the Way and the Truth so we are able to live for him so others can see him through us. Jesus showed us who God is, showing the example "so that they may have life and have it abundantly."[24] He did so because no matter how hard we try to get closer to God, the only way to do it is through faith in Jesus Christ.

In Jewish law (specifically in the Torah), each year the Jewish people would sacrifice a lamb on the eve of Passover (Friday), and then eat it on the first night of the holiday. Passover (which in Hebrew means Pesach) actually refers to the Passover lamb. Jesus made sure to accomplish every prophecy that was spoken of him by the prophets, that at times went into great detail. This next prophecy fulfillment, who I learned from Pastor Steven Furtick in his book, *Seven-Mile Miracle*, was brought to my attention. Back at the time of the Exodus, the Hebrews would use a stalk of hyssop to spread lamb's blood on their doorsteps as a sign for the Lord's spirit to pass over them. When Jesus had been on the cross for hours, he wanted a drink because he was thirsty. Now this was the second to last "word" that Jesus spoke, and goes far beyond what we think of when someone says, "they thirst." Jesus was in thirst to be with his Father in heaven before committing his Spirit into God's hands.[25] For an incredible explanation of not only Jesus's sixth "word" on the cross, but all of his last seven "words," I highly recommend reading Pastor Furtick's book. To provide more information on my last statement, it is clear Jesus didn't have to have a drink because he denied the first drink they offered him (which was wine and myrrh). Jesus was waiting to fulfill the last prophecy, which is in the book of Psalms and states, "They put gall in my food and gave me vinegar for my thirst."[26] Jesus was waiting to drink vinegar. What happens next will absolutely fire you up! Since he denied the first drink, the Romans then proceeded to take a sponge and stick it on a stalk of hyssop before dipping it in the wine vinegar that was also present. He allowed the wine vinegar to touch his lips, fulfilling the last prophecy. Back in the Hebrew Scriptures, the lamb's blood was splattered on the doorpost by using a stalk of hyssop so the Lord's Spirit would pass over them so they would be cleansed because it was a sign of purification. Jesus, God in the flesh, utilized hyssop and his blood on the Cross to purify mankind of their sins for all who repent. Jesus, being crucified on Friday (the eve of Passover), was the Passover Lamb!

Every single thing Jesus Christ did was for a reason. He wants to show us what to do when times are good, bad, and everywhere in between. He wants to show us how to live to the fullest with him, and he wants to show us how to coach others by coaching through you so you are able to have the greatest impact on people.

Earlier, I stated that he has been there from the beginning and will be there until the end. I wanted to show you through Scriptures that Jesus has been in the Old Testament since the beginning of Genesis. He was with Moses during the exodus, and he was with John on the island of Patmos after his resurrection, profoundly stating, "And behold, I am coming soon. Blessed is the one who keeps the words of the prophecy of this book."[27] I wanted to talk about Jesus being in Genesis (I only mentioned him once in the book of Genesis, but he is apparent many other times in the book. For example, please see Gen 3:15 which states, "He shall bruise your head, and you shall bruise His heel." This is referring to Jesus conquering death through his resurrection after being pierced[28] on his heel (and hands) during his crucifixion, and in revelation because these are the first and last books of the Bible. He was there at the beginning of time and is there in the future when he will come back while simultaneously being everywhere in between.

All this information brings me back to my statement earlier when I said that Jesus needed help. Through all the prophecies being fulfilled in the Old Testament and all his teachings in the New Testament, it is obvious that every move Jesus made was for a reason and every word he spoke was for us to learn from. I did not want to just state nonchalantly that he, God in the flesh, needed help. I wanted to give you the evidence, background, and facts through Scripture that Jesus intended to teach us something by needing Simon of Cyrene to help him.

Jesus constantly prayed to our Father in heaven without ceasing. He stated a parable in Luke 18 that meant to always pray and never lose heart.[29] In Jesus's darkest hour (in the garden of Gethsemane when the Romans came to arrest him), he prayed deeply. He sweated drops of blood because he was in such distress of knowing his destiny. Sweating blood is an actual condition and is called "hematidrosis." I cannot fathom the anxiety and pressure that Jesus must have felt during this time. But it is no coincidence that Jesus was in the garden of Gethsemane the night he was unnecessarily arrested. The word "Gethsemane" in Hebrew means "olive press" (i.e., the pressure or weight that he felt at that time). Jesus had his life's work planned from the very beginning (relating back to Gen 3:15 mentioned earlier).

In Jesus's hardest time in the garden of Gethsemane to the unfathomable pain he must have felt during his passion, he leaned on our Father. As he was nearing Golgotha, he needed help to carry his cross. He was showing us that we all need a Coach for support and we all need that person to keep us standing no matter what the circumstances may be. Jesus was showing us that we as coaches need to be there for who it is that leans on us in times of distress.

There is no better Man to follow as our personal coach than Jesus Christ, the Man that conquered death and stood from the beginning and will be with us to the end. There is no better Man to follow than God in the flesh, the one who stated, "Truly, I say to you, if you have faith like a grain of mustard seed, you will say to this mountain, 'Move from here to there,' and it will move, and nothing will be impossible for you."[30] We are all lost sheep and prodigal sons at times, and he allows us to constantly run back to him no matter what the circumstance (please see Luke 15 for parables).

I believe Jesus has given me such a Passion for him because I wanted to set my foundation in him and conquer something together. I didn't want to just know who Christ is, I wanted to *know* him, understand him, and live for him through something every day that we could do together so others can see him through me. And as previously stated, I believe that my eyes were truly opened in high school and God's plan all along for us was starting to take shape.

3—Paving the Way

DURING MY SENIOR YEAR, things started to change for me. Throughout the latter years of my high school career, I was a healthy kid but I was pretty skinny and weighed about 130 pounds at 5'9". I didn't have the desire to lift weights or work out at all. Now I was an athlete, as previously mentioned, but I didn't have the desire to build myself up through the utilization of weights. During my first three years of high school, internally my self-esteem was pretty low. I had friends and enjoyed high school, but I felt like something was missing inside me. As I truly looked to Jesus for guidance and help at this time, I pleaded to him, "I just want something to be Passionate about. I want us, together, to constantly strive for something every day. Whatever we do, I want us to be associated with some of the best, so people can see that you are the King and You are the One who got us there because of your living Passion in me."

Amazingly and surprisingly, as my senior year progressed, a fire started burning in me that made me want to start lifting weights. I got a membership to the LA Fitness that was close to our home in Indianapolis. Each morning at 5:30am, I would drive to the gym to swim laps for thirty minutes before school. I know you are probably thinking, "Why is Mike telling us he got up early to swim when he just mentioned lifting weights?" I know swimming steady laps for thirty minutes isn't going to pack on muscle, but I wanted to mention it because every day when I woke up to go to the gym, I felt something different. I desired to get up early and workout, my self-esteem increased, I was more talkative, and I felt a level of comfort within myself that I really have never felt before. I started to feel the presence of God more in my life and I felt a strong sense of purpose through what I started to take enjoyment in.

After school at around 2:30pm, I would crank the tunes in my '04 Grand Am (which I still have to this day; thank you, Mom and Dad, for that incredible car) and head to LA Fitness to go lift weights. When I say that I found enjoyment in lifting, boy do I mean it. Yes, I started lifting weights like most people and had a variation of some type of four-to-five-day split where I smashed back and biceps one day, chest and triceps the next, shoulders and traps the third, and crushed legs to the point where I couldn't sit down on the toilet the next day. But boy did I love it. I started to see some results and most importantly for me, I found serious enjoyment in something that I never would have thought. Honestly, in my first three years of high school, if you asked me for my list of the top fifty things I like to do for fun, lifting weights and having a purpose towards training wouldn't crack that list. Working out came out of nowhere, and it came after the desperation I had in prayer.

The winter was approaching and it was time for me to start applying to colleges. And yes, that absolutely included UCF. I applied early and made sure my grades were the best they could possibly be. I made sure to get recommendations from the teachers that knew me best and I was sure I was going to get my acceptance email from UCF early. Even though I thought it was a waste of time, my parents made me apply to other universities in Florida. As immature and ignorant as I was, I thought I knew my plan. I already knew I was going to UCF and I thought I had it all mapped out. I had great grades, I was a student athlete, I was in student council, and I had some serious volunteer hours. In addition, my sister was already going to UCF, which would help a lot in the application process. But as time passed, my acceptance letter never came. December was approaching and I still didn't hear back from any schools I applied to. I knew I would get in somewhere, but I was starting to get really nervous. My parents always helped me through that time because I ended up always venting to them about not having that official acceptance letter yet. But within my venting sessions, my parents said I should apply to Florida Atlantic University (FAU) as well. That was one of the few major universities I didn't apply to within Florida. I took their advice and applied but I knew I wouldn't hear back for at least a few weeks. But to be honest, UCF was still the only thing on my mind.

Unfortunately, as the days passed in December, I started to get some rejection letters from some universities in Florida. Yes, it was a bummer knowing I still don't have one acceptance letter when most of my friends already knew where they were going. But by trying to look at the positives, I still didn't get denied from UCF.

January came and I still neither got an email nor a physical letter in the mail. I then just took the initiative to call the admissions department at UCF to see the status of my application. The lady I spoke with was very nice, but all she told me was that a decision has been made and I should check my application portal. As I hung up the phone, I didn't know if I should feel excited with a decision being made or if I should feel incredibly nervous because she didn't tell me their decision. I suddenly didn't feel so confident that I would be going to UCF. With my heart rate possibly being over two hundred beats per minute, I started to log on to my portal to see the fate of my future.

Great anticipation was beginning to turn into horrendous anxiety as I waited for each page to load. I finally reached the place in my portal that read, "application decision." From my enormous desire to get into UCF, I checked the status of my application normally every business day and was used to my decision reading "application pending." But a decision had been made, and I clicked into the letter of notice. As you can expect, I did not get into UCF. I read that email over and over, hoping the words would change from the very polite rejection they gave me to "Congratulations on your acceptance into the University of Central Florida!" But the reality set in that I was not going to the school I wanted to most. In addition, I was also freaking out because I still didn't get accepted into a college at all yet. The only thing that I felt was inhibiting me from receiving an acceptance letter was my SAT scores. My standardized-test-taking skills were not stellar, but they certainly weren't bad and I felt that it shouldn't have resulted in receiving a rejection letter. I was sure that my great grades and all my extracurricular activities would make up for my average SAT scores.

After a disappointing conversation with my parents, I just wanted to get away and think about things. I wanted to go do something that would get my mind off school and this whole stressful application process. And of course, I went to go lift. Even today, which is years later, I still remember that drive to LA Fitness very vividly. I remember shouting out to God and asking him what was going on. At that time, I didn't understand any of this and I was emotionally frustrated. It was January and all my friends knew what their next steps in their life were going to be. I had great grades, a good extracurricular and athletic background, and a great reputation with my teachers so I could get outstanding recommendation from them. I felt confused, disappointed, and uncertain about my path for the future.

However, as my conversation with God continued, I started to feel an overwhelming presence over me during that drive. Yes, I had a lot of emotions running through my head at the time, but at the same time I felt an indescribable sense of peace. To be completely honest, I felt as if I had a security blanket over me. I knew God was with me at that point in time. I knew he was with me because I felt something different. As time has progressed for me, I am able to start to connect the dots and realize his path for me and how he's strategically paving it along the way. As previously mentioned, I vividly remember the night when I not just prayed for God, I was on my knees begging for him. I sought out God with my whole heart and with literally every ounce of me.

As the years' progress, I find myself getting deeper into the word every day. Recently, I was able to finish the good book and I can see what God was speaking through me at difficult moments in my life. I am starting to realize how he was coaching me through those difficult situations. As I look back at that confusing and frustrating time, I knew God was with me because he said in the book of Jeremiah, "Then you will call upon me and come and pray to me, and I will hear you. You will seek me and find me, when you seek me with all your heart."[31] The night when I first begged and pleaded for God, I knew he heard me. I knew he did because I begged for him with every ounce of me. I tried to seek him with all my heart and the more I now study the word, the more smiles get put on my face when I read over verses such as this and realize he was coaching me through those difficult times.

As my drive continued, I realized that everything was going to be alright. Through God's overwhelming presence with me at that time, I knew he had a plan. As bummed out as I was, I trusted him. During my senior year of high school, I put all my eggs in his basket. I wanted all of him. But at that young stage of my life, I thought it was all about me. I thought that by truly wanting and accepting him into my life, I could still stick to my plans. But as I grow older and wiser, that is certainly not the case. Committing your life to Jesus will lead you down the path of prosperity and true happiness, but along the way it may lead to some hard and confusing times. This is apparent when Jesus asked Peter, one of his disciples, when they had finished breakfast, "'Simon, son of John, do you love me more than these?' He said to him, 'Yes, Lord; you know that I love you.' He said to him, 'Feed my lambs.'"[32] Jesus proceeded to ask Peter two more times if he loved him, with Peter saying, "Yes, you know I love You." Jesus then said, "Truly, truly, I say to you, when you were young, you used to dress yourself and walk wherever you wanted, but when you are old, you will stretch out your hands, and another will dress you and carry you where you do not want to go."[33] During his talk with Peter, Jesus was referring to what kind of death he will be going through to glorify God. (Peter was crucified for spreading the gospel after Jesus appeared to him after his resurrection and ascended into heaven. It is believed that Peter was crucified upside down because he found himself unworthy to die the same way as Jesus.)

As I have previously mentioned, everything Jesus said and did was for a reason. It all relates to our lives and everything will turn out well in the end if we set him as our rock and foundation. I know some people may be saying to themselves, "I have been waiting a long time for that one break through moment to come, and it never has. I have tried to stay patient, but I cannot feel his plan for me right now." If this is you, please stay patient and stay constant in prayer.

In the book of Luke, chapter 18, Jesus talks about the parable of the persistent widow and how it resembles how God works with us. The parable talks about how a widow continually went to a judge day and night to seek justice against her adversity. The judge refused for quite some time, but after continuous persistence from her, he finally gave her justice so she would stop coming back to him. Near the end of his parable, Jesus said, "Hear what the unrighteous judge says. And will not God give justice to his elect, who cry to him day and night? Will he delay long over them? I tell you, he will give justice to them speedily. Nevertheless, when the Son of Man comes, will he find faith on earth?"[34] Keep hope and faith in your tough times, and he will bring you up in his time. Peter reminded us of this when he stated, "But do not overlook this one fact, beloved, that with the Lord one day is as a thousand years, and a thousand years as one day."[35] Waiting may seem like an eternity for us, but comfort and breakthrough will come in due time if we keep Jesus as our rock and personal coach.

As a mentor and coach, we must stay with our pupil through thick and thin and we as coaches must also stay with Jesus through thick and thin. He firmly expresses this in his parable of building your house on the rock. He told us,

> Everyone then who hears these words of mine and does them will be like a wise man who built his house on the rock. And the rain fell, and the floods came, and the winds blew and beat on that house, but it did not fall, because it had been founded on the rock. And everyone who hears these words of mine and does not do

them will be like a foolish man who built his house on the sand. And the rain fell, and the floods came, and the winds blew and beat against that house, and it fell, and great was the fall of it.[36]

When we commit our life to Christ, we must be all in. We have to accept the challenges that may arise from being a Christian. Jesus is our answer to everything and he will manifest himself to us if we keep his commandments[37] (which is loving God with all your heart, soul, and mind and loving your neighbor as yourself[38]). We all will face challenges in this life such as a family issue, financial struggle, temptation, or we find ourselves in a very dark place in life. But sticking with Jesus through it all is the key to our faith. "Faith is the assurance of things hoped for, the conviction of things not seen."[39] As brothers and sisters in Christ, "let us run with endurance the race that is set before us, looking to Jesus, the founder and perfecter of our faith, who for the joy that was set before Him endured the cross."[40] Scriptures tells us to be content with what we have. "For it is the Lord your God who goes with you. He will not leave you or forsake you."[41] So if you continue to keep your faith in him, as he will never leave you, and if you continue to be like the persistent widow who humbly begged for help day and night, while strongly desiring to have Jesus as your rock, he will raise you up in due time. As he stated, "Truly, truly, I say to you, whoever believes in me will also do the works that I do: and greater works than these will he do, because I am going to the Father. Whatever you ask in my name, this I will do, that the Father may be glorified in the Son. If you ask me anything in my name, I will do it."[42] He affirmed that he will lift you up more than ever if you continue to run the race with him with endurance. But as you can see in the previous verse, he said that we must abide by his standards first, which is doing the works that he did. These works center upon Jesus's greatest commandments which are loving God with all your heart, soul, mind, and strength, loving your neighbor as yourself, and loving one another as he loved us.[43] Jesus said that on these commandments depend all the Law and the Prophets. In Luke 10, a lawyer asked him how shall he inherit eternal life and Jesus responds by asking him how he interprets the law. The lawyer proceeds by stating Jesus' greatest commandments. Jesus then said to him, "You have answered correctly; do this, and you will live."[44] By accepting his grace and living through him, our tough times will turn out well for us because all things work together for good for those who love God.[45]

As I have learned more through Scripture as time proceeds, I can see how God was making me a stronger man through those confusing times. At the time when I was uncertain about my future and I didn't know what lay ahead, I knew I just had to trust in him. I had to trust his plans for us, not my own.

From understanding and accepting this, I was able to have an awesome workout and when I got home, my parents made me realize that I still didn't hear anything back from FAU yet. It hadn't crossed my mind that I still had other options besides UCF because initially I was so bummed out and set in my ways of only wanting to attend that school. But they were right and I knew God had a plan that was going to unfold very soon.

Sure enough, I found out that FAU had made a decision on my application a few days after my intimate conversation with God in that car ride and after the talk with my parents that proceeded. With overwhelming anticipation, I waited for my computer screen to fully load when I logged on. It seemed like an eternity considering how anxious I was. But sure enough, there it was. I got that acceptance letter I had been wanting for a long time. It legitimately felt like a two-hundred-pound weight vest was lifted off my shoulders. I ran downstairs to tell my mom and dad and they were pumped as well. I was ecstatic to know where I was going next and where I was going to start my college career. I was going to be a part of the FAU Owls family.

4—Rhymes and Reasons

THE LAST FEW MONTHS leading up to graduation were awesome. I was finally able to join in on the conversations that my friends had about college and the next journey in our lives. Even though most of them would be staying in Indiana for school, it was exciting to know that I was going to be a part of an awesome school such as FAU. It was pretty special to me because out of all the universities I applied to, FAU was the one that wanted me. They were the school that gave me a chance, so I was going to make the most of it and kick some hind tail. I determined that I was going to maintain a 4.0 GPA and get involved in some things that I really enjoyed. I couldn't wait for graduation and to make the drive down to Boca Raton, Florida with my parents to start classes. I was so fired up about getting down there that I decided to take summer classes that would start a few weeks after my high school graduation.

Before you know it, I was walking across that stage and receiving my high school diploma. Everybody was saying their goodbyes and after graduation was over, a switch flipped for me. The only thing on my mind after I walked out of the Indianapolis Convention Center with my parents was FAU and being the best student I could be so I could make a name for myself. This "new" Mike Roman had a different outlook on things. As I previously stated, I didn't have the greatest confidence in the world for my first three years in high school and my self-esteem was probably lower than most. Yes, I had a lot of friends and I enjoyed my time, but internally something was missing for me. But during my senior year and after graduation, I was ready to rock.

The next few weeks passed very quickly for me and it seemed like my parents and I were driving down to Florida literally the next day. They helped me get settled in, we said our goodbyes, and I was ready to start classes within the next few days. When I first met with my freshman counselor to discuss the route I wanted to take and what major I wanted to declare, I honestly didn't know exactly what I wanted to do. All I knew is that I wanted to wake up every day and truly enjoy what I do. I wanted to study something that I could continually get better at day after day. Even though I didn't know exactly what that was, I knew I wanted it to deal with the human body. Ever since I had desperation in prayer to Christ, I started lifting weights and pushing myself in ways I never had. Ultimately, I didn't know if I wanted to head more towards the medical route and declare as a biology major or more towards the kinesiology route and declare as an exercise science major. So I decided to stay undeclared, but I did register for multiple science classes pertaining to the human body outside of the general electives that I was required to take.

I am somewhat of a home body and moving about 1,100 miles away from where I lived for the past twelve years was tough. But starting that summer, I put the homesickness aside and worked my butt off. I ended up taking only two classes the first summer I was at FAU and I was able to get As in both of them. One of those classes was a US history course that was honestly one of the hardest classes I have ever taken. It seemed to me that I was studying day and night to understand all the material that was presented in the class. Typically, the summer terms in college are at an accelerated pace. This left me having to read an entire textbook in about eight weeks.

It was difficult for me because on top of that, the friends I did meet at FAU went to parties and other social gatherings a lot. Now, I am not the party type at all and personally, I love getting up before the sun comes up to get work done. If I wake up past 8:00 am, I normally feel like the whole day is wasted for me. I feel like I always have to get up early to study or do something that will give me a jump start to the day (like going to workout early in the morning). But at the same time, I still wanted to meet people and make new friends. I wanted to go out with them sometimes to just talk and relax and maybe meet a cute girl. But at the same time, I told myself that I was going to maintain a 4.0 GPA at FAU and be the best student I could. So, this left me staying in most nights studying US history because it is definitely not my best subject. Staying in and taking care of business was the best decision I made because I was able to keep up on my studies and I could get up early the next morning to go lift weights.

Fortunately, I was able to obtain a 4.0 GPA after my first semester and on top of that, I was doing some accessory studying of my own to learn more about weight lifting and training. With any extra time I had outside of studying for my actual classes, I had my head in any book or online article relating to strength and conditioning that I could get my hands on. This was my first time being exposed to periodization (which in lay terms means having a well thought out plan for improvement) and different programs. Gaining this knowledge allowed me to train with a purpose and I went into the gym every day with a plan. It was great for me because not only was I getting stronger, but I was putting on some size. As I said before, starting my senior year in high school, I weighed in at about 130 pounds at 5'9". As my senior year progressed and to the time my first semester at FAU had finished, I was close to 160 pounds! I felt good and my body was starting to fill in. When you feel good and when you feel like you look good, you play well and boy did I feel like I was playin' well.

The more I studied about the different philosophies and rhymes and reasons behind strength and conditioning, the more I became obsessed with it. I absolutely loved it. Anything I could get my hands on that related to strength and conditioning, I was reading it. As the fall semester approached, I decided I wanted to take action and head to FAU's Football Complex to see how I could get involved in their strength and conditioning department. The coaches I talked to were very knowledgeable and kind. They allowed me to be an intern for the fall semester, which absolutely fired me up. This was my first real experience with a collegiate strength and conditioning internship. Of course, it included the not-so-fun stuff like restocking the protein drink machine and cleaning the weight room. But I realized that in this industry, you have to pay some serious dues if you want to get anywhere, and being a brand new intern to this field, I had absolutely zero dues paid in the "dues jar." But at FAU, that is just a small thing I had to pay to not just be a part of it, but I got to learn from some insanely intelligent strength coaches. On top of that, I got to learn about other strength coaches within the industry when they referenced other brilliant minds.

When I first got to FAU, I felt like I found something special. I wanted to obtain and apply all the knowledge that I could regarding strength and conditioning. Backtracking to my senior year of high school until the end of my fall semester at FAU, I could say without a doubt that I grew up a lot. I grew so much mentally, physically, and spiritually. I was so fortunate to be a part of FAU and that phenomenal strength staff. But as time proceeded, it didn't seem like the place for me.

As I briefly discussed my time thus far at FAU, I did say that I was getting great grades, I was working out and getting stronger, and I was able to get an internship with the FAU strength and conditioning department. I was also reading like there was no tomorrow and was trying to be the best person I could be. But I did say that I didn't go out much because I was so focused on my studies and I'm not the party type. Yes, I was being a great student, but at the same time, I was beginning to get extremely lonely. I was then and I am now a very outspoken guy. Anyone who truly knows me without a doubt will probably say that I am one of the most talkative people they know. But near the midway point of my fall semester at FAU, I had an indescribable feeling inside that FAU wasn't the place for me.

As I have said before, the more I study the word, the more I am able to look back and see how God was coaching and teaching me along the way through his words. I tried as hard as I could with school and I stayed in prayer constantly, but everyone also needs a team. Whether that be friends or a spouse, everyone needs someone. Jesus demonstrated this by showing us that even he had a team of twelve that was with him all the time. They were with him when he performed his miracles, when he explained his parables about the kingdom of heaven, and after his resurrection, most of them preached the gospel all the way to the grave.

I knew FAU was a great stepping stone for me and I was able to grow in so many areas as well as learn about myself. I found out what I wanted to do with my life and I learned how to work hard. I found that I can attain anything that I set my mind to. Most importantly, I believe Christ put me in this situation because he wanted me to grow closer to him in prayer. A lot of nights, I would go on walks or runs to just be alone with God to find his presence. The peace I was able to find when I actively sought out his presence kept me going. I loved these walks or runs because they allowed me to be in solitude with him through prayer. When I felt like my tank was almost empty, he filled me back up to continue to keep going.

Jesus showed us his example of this when he would often withdraw to lonely places to pray.[46] He needed his operating system (God) to keep him going. Jesus proceeded to perform some of his greatest miracles after being in solitude with his Father. For example, in Matt 14, Jesus was accompanied by a great crowd. He dismissed the crowds and asked his disciples to get in a boat and go before him to the other side of the lake (Sea of Galilee). He then went up to the mountain by himself to pray. While Jesus was in solitude with God, the disciples felt like they were alone as they battled a raging storm and winds in the boat. However, when they felt alone, Jesus appeared, walking on the sea towards them. Peter, not knowing if it was Jesus or not, said, "Lord, if it is You, command me to come to You on the water." Jesus said, "Come." Peter proceeded to walk on the water towards Jesus until he cast his eyes away from him and gazed upon the storm that was present. He began to sink and he cried out, "Lord, save me!" Jesus proceeded by reaching out his hand to take hold of him, saying, "O you of little faith, why did you doubt?" When they both got into the boat, the winds then ceased." Those in the boat proceeded to worship him, saying, "Truly you are the Son of God."[47]

Not only is Jesus showing us that we need to be in solitude with God (please refer back to Luke 5:16), but he is showing us God performs his greatest miracles after we feel alone or are lonely if we keep our faith in him. Notice that when the disciples needed a miracle, Jesus appeared to them. But when Peter looked at the storm that was present, he began to sink until he refocused his attention on Jesus. If you are in a tough and lonely situation, try as best as you can to follow his example. Rejoice always, pray without ceasing, and give thanks in all circumstances. God will reward those who diligently search for Him.[48]

Know that God is always with you in lonely times and he will manifest himself to those who love him and earnestly seek him (please refer back to John 14:21). Please take note of where Jesus performed his miracle of walking on water, the Sea of Galilee. Amazingly, this body of water is the lowest freshwater lake on earth, approximately seven hundred feet below sea level. Jesus performed many of his miracles at the Sea of Galilee, some of which include the healing of the lame, the blind, the crippled, the mute, and many others, as crowds put them at his feet, and he healed them.[49] He even performed the miracle of the feeding of the five thousand off the shore of the Sea of Galilee. It was no coincidence that Jesus performed all these miracles at the lowest freshwater lake in the world. Jesus was indirectly telling us that he will be with us in our lowest point. He is clearly telling us that when you are lonely and when you have a heavy burden, he will turn your desperation, loneliness, and troubles into blessings beyond your wildest dreams. However, the miracles that I described all have one necessary trait in common. They all came from obedience and faithfulness that is required to please God. "Without faith, it is impossible to please him."[50] Yes, we can absolutely run back to him when we need him and he will always accept us (please see the parable of the lost sheep and the parable of the lost coin in Luke 15), but we must stick with him through thick and thin as he will always be there for us and he will reward those who are faithful to him.[51]

I wanted to provide this background about Jesus in hopes that you can apply it to any situation you are currently in or have been in and how you can utilize these teachings for future situations that may arise. Whether that be as a parent with your children, as a coach with your athletes, or as a mentor and your pupil, keeping your faith in him at all times is the foundational and essential element to his other teachings. Once our eyes are truly opened to him, we may then see that what he teaches is for a greater purpose. By no means am I perfect. There are days when I feel like I'm doing a lot of things right, but there are more days when I completely mess up. But through everything I do, I attempt to stay faithful in Jesus because I want to always live my life for him and coach through him.

5—*Trusting the Process*

WHEN I GOT TO the point when I felt extremely lonely at FAU, it was time to go home for Thanksgiving break. But instead of driving back up to Indianapolis to spend the time with just my parents and sister, we decided to have Thanksgiving in Knoxville, Tennessee with my extended family because that is where a good portion of my cousins, aunts, and uncles live. It is always great to round up the whole family and spend it together at such a special time. The food is fantastic, Thanksgiving NFL football never fails, and we can have great conversations about what is going on in our lives.

During the quality time I was able to spend with my family, I found myself talking to my cousin. We were just talking about life and what was new on his end and mine. He was asking me about FAU and what I was studying. I told him that I found out what I wanted to do with my life. I told him about the enjoyment and excitement I got about being in the weight room and how pumped up I would get when the football team was slammin' bars and absolutely gettin' after it in the early mornings before class. I told him how I loved the meticulous nature of the strength and conditioning profession and how I loved studying the human body from so many different aspects (e.g., anatomical, biomechanical, and physiological). I loved learning more about the anatomy and biomechanics of the body so I could fully grasp how the body should properly move and what musculature is being utilized and how it relates to the athlete's sport from an injury preventative standpoint and improvement in force production. I was obsessed with learning different methods that strength and conditioning coaches were using across the country to improve their athletes and how it all added up to being a part of something special. I probably went way more in depth than what he was looking for, but whenever someone wants to talk about sports performance, I give them the whole thing. But I also told him as much as I loved learning and improving in the field of sports performance, I didn't think FAU was for me. I told him how thankful I am to be a part of FAU, but I wanted to be at a place that I could consider home.

My cousin then proceeded to tell me, "Man, I am so happy you found something you love. I need to connect you with Johnny Long, he can steer you in the right direction." At the time, I knew of Coach Long, but the more I researched about him and the University of Tennessee, the more fired up I got! Coach Long was a part of the Phillip Fulmer era when the Volunteers were able to have incredible seasons (including a BCS National Championship in 1998) with some of the best and most hardworking players the University of Tennessee has ever seen such as Peyton Manning, Al Wilson, Inky Johnson, and Tee Martin.

Coach Long departed from the University of Tennessee with Coach Fulmer after the 2008 season and then proceeded to open his own performance facility called "Johnny Long's Training Academy (JLTA)." JLTA was a great facility that contained everything you would need to train as an athlete. The weight room had nine platforms, multiple sets of dumbbells that ran up to a hundred pounds, and other accessory equipment to ensure you could perform all your sport specific movements. On top of that, there were two turf, full-sized soccer fields outside (one was covered by an awning to create an indoor feel) where you could get your resisted or unresisted speed work in. He and his staff trained a wide range of people at various ages with different skill levels. A myriad of club and school teams came to train there, including football, baseball, softball, rugby, and basketball to name a few. The facility was home to the Knoxville Soccer Academy, which included multiple teams ranging from ages eight to eighteen. Also, there were many fitness classes available to the public that ranged from early in the mornings at 5:30 am to the evening groups at 6:00 pm. On top of all this, the weight room had six huge garage doors you could open to create an outdoor feel to let the fresh air in during the spring through fall time. This allowed the athletes to go straight from the weight room to the field to run, or from doing plyometric movements outside to coming in and doing some explosive weight-lifting variations.

When I found out all these things that were offered at JLTA, I thought to myself, "Man, I could get so much experience if I could work for Johnny." In addition, I could learn from one of the best strength coaches to ever do it. (Coach Long is a part of the Gayle Hatch coaching tree and has produced some of the best strength coaches in collegiate and professional sports.)

Normally, I don't put all my eggs in one basket, but when I feel like something is God's plan, I put all my eggs in his basket plus some. After long talks with God in prayer while I was at FAU, I felt like what my cousin presented to me was a huge window of opportunity.

After discussing this with my parents, I reached out to Johnny and he gave me the opportunity to be an intern for him starting in the summer of 2013. Once I got confirmation that I was able to work for him that next summer, I decided to put all my eggs in this basket. Honestly, the situation couldn't have been better for me at the time because I would have a place to live as well. My Aunt Shelly and Uncle Bob said I could stay at their house in Knoxville during the summer!

Once Thanksgiving break was over and after the fall semester, I researched more into the University of Tennessee (UT) and what it had to offer. With me obviously developing a greater enjoyment for strength and conditioning and sports performance as time progressed at FAU, I decided to look into UT's kinesiology major within the education department. It seemed like a phenomenal opportunity and after further discussing with my parents, we happily agreed upon applying to transfer to UT. My parents were just as excited as I was because they really wanted to move to Knoxville. This situation seemed like a no-brainer for my family and I because I could further pursue what I truly enjoyed, my parents could move to an area that they loved, and if I got into UT, I would be able to have in-state tuition via my parents move to Knoxville. As a family, we confirmed our plans with each other and the application process that I thoroughly loved (sarcasm) started all over again.

As compared to my application process during high school, the situation with UT was way less stressful. Since I was applying to be a transfer student, I did not have to go through the many steps that high school students were required to. All I had to do was simply fill out the necessary personal information about myself and submit my official transcripts from FAU. Fortunate for me, I didn't have to submit my standardized test scores. Again, I didn't do bad on my SAT's, but like I said, I'm not the best standardized test taker and I was near the 50th percentile. If I had to submit these scores, I most likely would have been ruled out in the application process. (Did I mention that I took the SAT three times in high school to try and improve my score?) However, as I described to you earlier, I committed myself to obtaining a 4.0 GPA while I was at FAU, and I got it. So, with me only having to supply my official transcripts from FAU to UT, there was no doubt in my mind that I was going to be a Volunteer considering they were only judging me off one solid criteria (my transcript).

Early within the spring semester of 2013, I found out my application decision from UT. Sure enough, I did get accepted and I was going to be a Tennessee Volunteer starting in the fall. When I found out, I was so jacked up! It really seemed like everything was coming together. I immediately called my parents and my sister Chelsea to tell them. They were just as ecstatic as I was! And of course, what is a guy like me going to do when he is super pumped and wants to blow off some steam? Go lift weights or run! Or, why not both?

The lift I had was fantastic, but more importantly for me was the run that proceeded. I vividly remember that run and thinking to myself, "Boy are things starting to come together." While on that run, I remember looking back at the journey God and I have had thus far. I'll never forget pleading and begging for more of him in high school. From that point until now I finally connected the dots. I firmly believe that the Lord wanted me to be at the University of Tennessee (which I will further describe a little later), and it all started by going to FAU. If I ended up getting into UCF, I know for certain that I would never have considered transferring to Tennessee. And if I never went to FAU, I wouldn't have obtained that 4.0 GPA because I had so much extra time to study due to the lonesomeness at times.

From my experience, what I am trying to explain is that God has a reason for every situation he puts you in. My goal of explaining my journey to you is not to tell you about myself. My goal is to explain my path in hopes that you relate it to your experiences, troubles, and triumphs and know that your path all relates to the rhymes and reasons within God's word. He knows the plans he has for us, "plans for welfare and not for evil, to give [us] a future and a hope."[52]

Ecclesiastes 3 tells us that there is a reason for everything. There is "a time to break down, and a time to build up; . . . a time to tear, and a time to sew."[53] Within our journey with him, there is a time for growth and a time where it seems like we are lost. We have to trust the process. Whether that be with your athletic program, your child, or your student, you must be willing to accept the prosperous times and the times that seem unfruitful. We need to be patient as best as we can in all circumstances. This is made known to us in Gal 6 which states, "And let us not grow weary of doing good, for in due season we will reap, if we do not give up."[54] I want to state this because in our journey with God we will experience ups and downs.

We will experience fruitful and unfruitful times. But by keeping Christ as your rock in all circumstances, you will develop into a better coach with whatever it is you do. I can attest to this from my experience that I have described. In order for us to be the best coaches we can within Christ, we must always keep him as our foundation, and that is something that I continually try to work on every day. If he is our rock and foundation, his principles and teachings will follow for us. God saves the best for last.

6—Run the Race to Win

THE SPRING SEMESTER AT FAU flew by and before I knew it, I was on my way to Knoxville, Tennessee. I was ready to take on the next stopping point within my journey thus far. I was ready to learn and attempt to build upon my craft as an aspiring strength and conditioning coach. Given all that JLTA had to offer, I knew I could get experience in multiple areas as well as get my own training in at a really cool facility. Taking on this next challenge was going to be fun, and I wanted to make the most of it.

My first week at JLTA was amazing. It seemed that my aspiration to learn about strength and conditioning programming and the rhymes and reasons behind everything increased exponentially. All I wanted to do was train, learn new material and methods, and then apply it in real world coaching. I wanted to show Coach Long and the staff that this is what I wanted to do with my life. I wanted to be the first one to show up and the last person to leave. I came to work every morning at 5:00 am and didn't leave until 7:00 pm most days. You would think that fourteen-hour work-days would be horrendous, but I enjoyed every minute of it. My enjoyment for this field increased so much during my time at JLTA that summer. I was trying to make the most out of my time there because I felt God's plan was continuing to be revealed to me more every day. Colossians 3 tells us to set our minds on things above, not on things of this earth, and whatever we do, do everything in the name of the Lord Jesus.[55] Whatever type of coach you are, a parent, a teacher, a manager, or a strength coach, we know that God has utilized us in this way to fulfill a greater purpose through him. If we see the bigger purpose and do everything through him, Christ will manifest himself not only to you in a greater way, but he will be manifested to others because they will be able to see Christ through you. Once we find true enjoyment in our coaching through him, we will appreciate what it is we do even more because it has a greater purpose. After all, Jesus tells that we must love one another as he loved us and to make disciples of all nations by spreading his gospel.[56]

As will be described later within this book, Jesus presented his teachings and miracles with compassion and grace, but He was also very firm when he needed to be. For example, as Matt 16 articulates, "Jesus began to show his disciples that he must go to Jerusalem and suffer many things from the elders and chief priests and scribes, and be killed, and on the third day be raised. And Peter took him aside and began to rebuke him, saying, 'Far be it from you, Lord! This shall never happen to you.' But he turned and said to Peter, 'Get behind me, Satan! You are a hindrance to me. For you are not setting your mind on the things of God, but on the things of man.'"[57] I don't know about you, but I would be pretty afraid if God in the flesh said that to me. What I am stating is that as a Coach in Christ, we must still be very firm when need be because people who love you are responsible for giving constructive criticism when necessary. Jesus is showing us that we must be firm, fair, and friendly in our approach so we can build up and strengthen who it is we are coaching. And by this love, we can hopefully open the eyes of others so they can see him through us, which is ultimately what Jesus wants.

By trying to give my all for him every day, I started to feel his presence more in everything I did. Whether that be reading, lifting weights, or coaching, I wanted to do it all for him. As time progressed, my appreciation and gratefulness towards him allowed my enjoyment of strength and conditioning to turn into my Passion. I firmly believe in my heart that desiring to go for him every day has opened other doors for me. As I said earlier, I desired to be associated with some of the best strength coaches in the world, and he has surrounded me around some great company. While maintaining a great relationship with Coach Long, I had the opportunity to be a full-time intern at the University of Tennessee for Herman Demmink III, who at the time was the strength coach for the baseball and tennis teams at UT. I personally think he is one of the most intelligent strength coaches in the world and I am fortunate enough to consider him one of my best friends. He taught me an immense amount, and I am incredibly fortunate to have met him.

After graduation, I was able to meet the head strength coach for the Washington Nationals through a mutual friend which eventually led to an internship with their Major League club. During my time in Washington DC, I was able to learn from some of the best coaches, therapists, and physicians in the world, and I am extremely grateful to them for allowing me to be a part of their organization for the time I was with them.

Following that season, I found myself in a situation where I didn't know what lay ahead. I felt as if my journey came to a sudden stop. That winter, I was in a situation that left me questioning what my next move should be. All of these questions led me to long conversations in prayer and I struggled to find where he wanted us. I knew the Lord led me to all of these incredible coaches and people for a reason, but I was struggling to find out what would be next for us.

As I found myself in this situation of uncertainty, I still knew that God had a rhyme and a reason for it. I knew Jesus was my foundation and my rock, and I knew his plan would continue to prosper by staying patient in him. Scripture tells us, "Blessed is the man who trusts in the Lord, whose trust is the Lord. He is like a tree planted by water, that sends out its roots by the stream, and does not fear when heat comes, for its leaves remain green, and is not anxious in the year of drought, for it does not cease to bear fruit."[58] No matter what situation we are in, if Jesus is our rock and our trust, he will bring us through. Confusing times and misunderstandings will arise, but we must stay patient in tribulation and constant in prayer.[59] The book of Proverbs says, "Trust in the Lord with all your heart, and do not lean on your own understanding. In all your ways acknowledge him, and he will make straight your paths."[60] In life, God will place us where he wants us to be and he will raise us up in due time if we trust him. Just look at David. David was a young shepherd before God anointed him to defeat Goliath with just a sling and a stone and be king of Israel. As a shepherd, he served his current assignment and was anointed in God's perfect timing.

If we set our trust in him, serve our current assignment, give everything we have for him every day (please refer back to Col 3:17), and stay patient in him when times seem bleak while understanding that his reasoning is for a greater purpose, he will raise us up to ultimately make us stronger members in Christ. I continued to push and trust this process when I didn't know what was next. All I knew was that whatever lay ahead for me, I prayed that it would allow me to become a better man of faith. I remember during that time of uncertainty, I asked God to put me on a path that leads me closer to him.

Sure enough, in late December, Johnny Long called me and said that he took the director of sports performance role at Carson Newman University, which is a Christian University in Jefferson City, Tennessee and is about forty minutes east of Knoxville. He offered me a graduate assistant position within the department where I would train various sports teams while having the opportunity to get my master's degree paid for. I was so incredibly humbled and honored for this position to be offered to me. I was going to have the opportunity to go back to school starting in January and I was going to be able to work within my Passion. In addition, I could save money and live with my parents since they made the transitional move to Knoxville when I transferred to UT. My graduate assistant position was finalized and the next stop within the journey had arrived.

When January came, the early morning grind began. Considering we had 6:00 am lifting sessions every day (whether it be for football or one of my Olympic-based sports), I had to be up at 4:15 am, get everything ready, and then make the forty-minute commute to Jefferson City. As a staff, we had to be thirty minutes early to make sure everything was set up so we were ready to rock 'n' roll by the time 6:00 rolled around. Our last sessions would end around 6:00 pm and then I would head home, make food for the next day, and do it all over again. But you know what, I loved every minute of it. I loved every minute of it because I was coaching for a greater purpose. I was coaching for Christ. I just mentioned that during my time of uncertainty before I had the opportunity at Carson Newman, I asked God to lead me on a path that would draw me closer to him. In front of the Ken Sparks Athletic Complex (which includes the weight room) at Carson Newman, there is an enormous cross that is displayed right in front. This beautiful Cross stands approximately fifteen-feet tall and it oversees a gorgeous waterfall. My path of driving forty minutes every morning to Carson Newman literally led me to Jesus every day. I still get emotional every time I think about it. Not only did I drive up to him every day, but I was able to have Bible study sessions with the staff on a regular basis. The staff included me, Coach Long, and Thomas Collins. Not only is Johnny Long one of the great strength coaches within the industry, but Thomas Collins is one of the most brilliant, hardworking, and diligent coaches out there. I've previously said that I wanted to be associated with the best strength coaches in the country. Not only was God leading me on a path closer to him, but he was also putting me in positions to be associated with some of the best coaches to learn from.

The year I spent at Carson Newman was the best year of my life thus far. During my time at Carson Newman, my faith and love for Jesus grew exponentially and I was able to draw even closer to him by reading all of his word. It allowed me to further connect the dots within my path and it made me realize even more that the Passion God gave me has such a greater purpose. He clearly showed me at Carson Newman that he is with me. he showed me that he is the Alpha and the Omega, the Beginning and the End, the Great I AM, and our Gateway to Glory.

As previously mentioned, my goal of describing my journey to you was to not plainly tell you about myself. My goal was to explain my path so you can relate it to your Passion, triumphs, and troubles in hopes that you can see God is always with you no matter what and he will manifest himself to you in ways you cannot imagine if you set Jesus as your foundation and rock. I wanted to give you my experiences thus far because it is the way I know best to hopefully spread his gospel and word. My hope is that you can relate your journey to mine and the given teachings in Scripture throughout the book thus far. My hope is that I demonstrated to you that Jesus needs to be our foundation if we want to truly be coaches in Christ, and this is something that we can build upon every day. If we don't have the foundation set, the house will crumble. From the book thus far, you can see that I have been running a race that has included multiple bumps, hills, valleys, and triumphs.

One of my favorite verses to live by is written by the apostle Paul and states, "Do you not know that in a race all the runners run, but only one gets the prize? Run in such a way as to get the prize."[61] I want you to conceptually apply this verse as the base for the rest of this book. As I mentioned, if we want to coach for Christ, he must be our personal coach. With that being said, we will be running the race and his teachings will help guide us along the way as we strive to coach like him. Throughout each proceeding chapter, I will provide coaching points from him and describe how we can utilize his ministry to help glorify him through our coaching. With that being said, let's get warmed up and ready to go, because we have a race to run.

Part II—The Coach Within

KNOWING THAT WE MUST first have Jesus as our rock and foundation, we are now able to dive into his ministry and see how he operated as a coach. It is my hope that by doing so, you can take his teachings and utilize them to the fullest so you are able to have a more fruitful and prosperous coaching path. I want to take you along some points within Jesus's ministry to the best of my ability so you can see how he operated to ultimately become the best coach and mentor this world has ever seen and will ever know. It is my hope that by setting him as your rock and identity, you will always look to him for guidance along your eternal path of being brothers and sisters in Christ. After all, he was, is, and will always be. We can always look to him for advice. This is what he wants from us. He desires to be our coach on a daily basis, willing to give us the true peace and validation that we so desire. We all desire validation. We as humans look to this in many ways that may come in the form of seeing how many Facebook or Instagram likes we get or by how much money we make, for example. As Christian coaches, we must first try to improve upon seeking true validation, which is from God. Finding validation through success is a great way to keep improving, and we should always try to be the best we can be. But when we realize that true satisfaction comes from the validation we receive from God when we commit our work to him, eternal satisfaction is made known to us. As it is written,

> So we, though many, are one body in Christ, and individually members of one another. Having gifts that differ according to the grace given to us, let us use them: if prophecy, in proportion to our faith; if service, in our serving; the one who teaches, in his teaching; the one who exhorts, in his exhortation; the one who contributes, in generosity; the one who leads, with zeal; the one who does acts of mercy, with cheerfulness.[62]

We can see through Paul's words that in order to efficiently coach for Christ, we must realize that it is for a greater purpose and our validation in what we do needs to be for him. We graciously receive validation from God by setting him as our identity and committing ourselves to him. Jesus did exactly this before he began his ministry. He wanted to show us that we must first commit to him before anything else. He sought to find validation from God because he wanted his works to be for the greater purpose.

In order to start the race and our neverending journey of coaching for Christ, I believe we must adopt key attributes that Jesus exhibited. I believe we must first be transformed through him so we can coach and positively affect others for him. Before his ministry, (in our case, coaching path) he first committed himself and then surrounded himself around people that would be able to help him. He then proceeded to perform incredible miracles and wonders through having a servant mindset. While committing his life to servitude, he also continuously taught us how to live so we can continuously let our Passion shine through God.

Within Part II, I want to discuss keys attributes that we should adopt within ourselves before we can effectively coach for Christ for our entire lives. I believe we must mimic key things that Jesus did throughout his life so we may be changed from the inside out, which will better help us to coach like him. As previously stated, Jesus first committed himself to God. He then surrounded himself around people that were able to help him throughout his ministry. He continually lived his life through prayer while maintaining his driving force, God. I want to discuss each aspect in detail first, which I believe will help us write the "Tablets of a Coach's Heart" within us, which is discussed in chapter 11. Let us start our coaching journey through Jesus's first act of servitude, commitment.

7—Establishing Your Coaching Identity through Commitment

WE CAN SEE THAT Jesus first committed himself and sought out validation from God by getting Baptized. Jesus encouraged John the Baptist to baptize him by saying, "Let it be so now, for thus it is fitting for us to fulfill all righteousness." Jesus was then baptized, and when he came out of the water, the heavens opened and he saw the Spirit of God descend on him like a dove to rest on him. Then, a voice from heaven said, "This is my beloved Son, with whom I am well pleased."[63] We need to take note and read into what Jesus did. I would like to give thanks to Pastor Steven Furtick for clearly pointing this out to me via a sermon. Jesus first obeyed God by getting baptized. For Jesus said, "Truly, truly, I say to you, unless one is born of water and the Spirit, he cannot enter the kingdom of God."[64] Once Jesus ascended from the water, the dove came down. We can see that once Jesus obeyed the word of God, he received validation.

Jesus is showing us that once he submitted to the foundational element of setting God as his identity, he experienced justification for the greater purpose. It is not until after Jesus was baptized did he then perform his wondrous works and miracles in the Gospels. After we have set our identity in Christ, we are then able to coach with a new passion, a new enjoyment, a new fire, and a new energy because we know that what we are doing has a new meaning. Once he is set as our identity, our passion for coaching can be taken to a different level. As it is written, "He died for everyone so that those who receive his new life will no longer live for themselves. Instead, they will live for Christ, who died and was raised for them."[65] Once we commit to him and desire to seek validation from the Man above, we can truly live and coach for him with a new passion. This relates back to Rom 12:5–8, which is written above. Once he is our identity, we are able to lead with enthusiasm, provide acts of mercy with cheerfulness to whom it is we are a coach for, and help serve others in a new way so they can reach their true potential.

Jesus also expressed the mindset that we as coaches must develop and exhibit in order to see long-term prosperity and fulfillment once we commit. Throughout his teachings, he expressed, "but lay up for yourselves treasures in heaven, where neither moth nor rust destroys and where thieves do not break in and steal. For where your treasure is, there your heart will be also."[66] As a coach and leader, we all at some point have developed a strategic plan that puts our mentees in the best possible position to succeed. Whether it is giving someone advice, creating a plan with an end goal that shows a steady progression, or developing them to be a leader in the future. To lead and coach for Christ, it is important that our guidance to others comes from the higher purpose.

As I have previously mentioned while describing my current coaching path with Christ, when I was younger I always knew Jesus, but I didn't feel that my heart was changed through him until I had desperation and sought him out with all I had. Within the Gospels, Jesus states that we must deny ourselves and take up our cross and follow him daily.[67] In order to effectively coach for him, we have to be changed through him. This essentially means that we must be all in with Jesus. Through our ups and downs, hills and valleys, triumphs and troubles, he must be our foundation. I would like to reiterate that Jesus said we must "deny ourselves" and follow him daily. By denying our self, we must put away the things that are holding us down and set our standard for what really matters as we go through life. For example, do you let money or materialistic things hold you down? Do you let continuously pleasing other people hold you down? This is something that we all as humans struggle with. As I have said before, "Some days I feel like I get it right, but most days I feel that I'm at the opposite end and I'm doing everything wrong." Even Paul, the author of much of the New Testament, states in Rom 7, "For I know that nothing good dwells in me, that is, in my flesh. For I have the desire to do what is right, but not the ability to carry it out. For I do not do the good I want, but the evil I do not want is what I keep on doing."[68] This is an example and proof that we cannot be perfect. That is the beauty of grace. "God shows his love for us in that while we were still sinners, Christ died for us."[69] But if we believe that the world has been crucified to us, and us to the world, and "if we have died with Christ, we believe that we will also live with him."[70] Having this desire and Passion in your heart displays faith in Jesus, by which we are justified and we have peace with God.

This essential element must be ingrained in us and is something that I desire to work on every day. If we don't have this foundation, it will be easier to fall away. Our essential element will not stop us from seeing distractions that try to pull us away from him. But it will make our path clearer and it will assist us in maintaining our integrity and steadfastness as we look to influence and coach others in the right way. If you are still reading along through this book and you have been asking Jesus into your heart, I deeply hope you pray the following prayer. If you are experiencing a time in which you believe in Jesus and you trust in him, but you don't know how to commit to him or where to start, I hope we can change that today, together. It is my hope that by praying this prayer, you sincerely open your heart to him and will be changed through him so you may be able to live and serve for him, in which we are all called to do. I hope you may pray along with me as you ask Christ into your heart.

> *Jesus, my brother, my defender, my counselor, and my refuge. With all my heart and with all my soul, I ask that you come into my heart. I confess that you, Jesus, are Lord and I believe in my heart that God raised you from the dead. Have your way in me Jesus. Please open my eyes to see, my ears to hear, and my heart to understand you more and please draw me closer to you every day. I want to fully commit my life to you and serve for you so I may live for the greater purpose. Make me become more dependent on you every day so I may continue down your path for me and protect me from becoming led astray. I know that I am not perfect, but I want you and I need you. Please Jesus, be my Shepherd. I humbly ask that you make me one of your sheep. Lead and guide me as to where you want me to go so we can experience the true fruits of life, together. Please be my rock, my foundation, and my fortress because with you, I cannot be shaken. Allow me to be a branch from you as the vine and mold me into who you want me to become. Please, manifest yourself to me and no matter what, always keep my eyes on you. When storms come, please continue to be my rock and keep me walking in your light so I may not stumble. You are the Way, the Truth, and the Life. I am nothing without you and I ask that we start and continue our journey together, so others may see You through me. In Your Name I pray Jesus, Amen.*

Whether Jesus has been your life or whether you asked him into your life for the first time, it is my hope that you always remain committed to him and you allow him to abide within you. When I fully committed my life to Jesus, and the deeper I longed to be a part of him, I realized that I couldn't and didn't want to live without him. And because I have the passionate desire to give my absolute best for his calling for me (serving as a strength and conditioning coach), I realize that our potential is unmeasurable. By committing to him and realizing the power that God possesses through us if we allow him to change our hearts, our capacity to thrive while positively influencing others is limitless. I can attest to this firsthand. From going to a very skinny kid and not knowing what I wanted to accomplish or do in life, to developing an indescribable Passion of serving Jesus as a strength and conditioning coach, I can wholeheartedly say that I have been able to influence men and women in a positive way by seeing them grow as better athletes and people through the joy and indescribable fire that burns in my heart from coaching.

And in time, I have realized that committing to Jesus is only the beginning. I have found out through different experiences that by committing to being a Christian and by fully devoting your life to Jesus, this world tries to pull you back to it. Peter challenges us to hold fast to what we believe in by saying, "Be sober-minded; be watchful. Your adversary the devil prowls around like a roaring lion, seeking someone to devour. Resist him, firm in your faith, knowing that the same kinds of suffering are being experienced by your brotherhood throughout the world."[71] Peter expressed to us to not be surprised at trials that come upon us to test us, as though something strange were happening to us.[72] He then goes onto say that once we have suffered and resisted certain circumstances or situations that try and hold us down, God will "restore, confirm, strengthen, and establish" us.[73] I wanted to mention this as the next coaching point from Jesus within our race, which is to resist temptation and remain committed to him through trials and tribulation.

As I have mentioned, once Jesus committed to God through his baptism, and was with the Spirit, he was then tested through much temptation. As he was led up into the wilderness by the Spirit to be tempted by the devil, Jesus proceeded to fast for forty days and forty nights. Being extremely hungry, the tempter came and said to him, "If you are the Son of God, command these stones to become loaves of bread." But he answered, "It is written, 'Man shall not live by bread alone, but by every word that comes from the mouth of God.'"[74]

What I believe Jesus meant by this is that everything we do needs to be centered around God and his commandments, which we know is to love one another, just as he loved us and to love God with all your heart, soul, mind, and strength. If we abide by these two commandments to the best of our ability and allow him to transform our hearts through his love, then we will be able to recognize what is right and wrong and live with him seven days a week, 365 days a year. Jesus doesn't want us to just recognize him and be with him on Sundays. He wants to reign in your heart and be with you every minute of the day.

Through this temptation, Jesus is also directly showing that we must exhibit patience and persistence in our tough times. I don't know about you, but if I didn't eat for forty straight days, I would want to eat anything in sight. But through this extremely tough time for him, he remained steadfast to his faith by continuing to push through even when times are hard. We are able to relate Jesus' first temptation in the wilderness to so many challenges that we face in life, especially as it relates to serving and coaching others.

One of the most inspirational figures in my life is a man named Inky Johnson. Inky played football at the highest level at the University of Tennessee (UT) at the time when one of my mentors, Johnny Long, was the head strength coach at UT. Inky was a projected first-round draft pick in the NFL before suffering a devastating injury that caused his right arm to be paralyzed, which sadly ended his football career. However, Inky never gave up and he has become the most inspirational and motivating speaker I have ever heard. I can honestly say that tears come to my eyes every time I hear this man speak because of the Passion that he shows. He is not only full of incredible wisdom, but his integrity to what he does and what he stands for is unprecedented. I highly recommend that you read his amazing book, *Inky Johnson: An Amazing Story of Faith and Perseverance*, which describes his life's journey and how he has overcome incredible obstacles which has resulted in positively influencing other people's lives.

I wanted to mention Inky because he is the epitome of what staying strong looks like when things get incredibly hard or if our life drastically changes. Inky has mentioned that his life has revolved around Jer 29:11 which reads, "For I know the plans I have for you, declares the Lord, plans for welfare and not for evil, to give you a future and a hope." Inky has said in relation to this verse, in a quote attributed to him, that "I feel like I'm living that plan out. The things that happen to us in life were not designed to stop us. They're designed to reposition us so we can come into contact for what God really has for us. So, everything that I do, I do to honor God." Inky is a living testimony and an example of what a coach in Christ is. God transformed and repositioned Inky into what he ultimately wanted him to do, which was to influence others' lives in a positive way. Not only has he positively influenced and changed people's lives, but he has done it the right way, which is through honoring God and carrying out his purpose.

Inky also lives by a certain method that he terms "Empty the bucket." This essentially means that he gives everything he has in all that he does every day for the greater purpose. He says that he carries a bucket around everywhere he goes. He means that he is working around the clock, 365 days a year for the greater purpose. He is honoring God in everything he does, all the time.

By living by every word that comes from the mouth of God, I believe we can refer to what Jesus said as to why he spoke in parables, which is, "lest they should see with their eyes and hear with their ears and understand with their heart and turn, and I would heal them."[75] Through the previous quote from Inky, it is clear that he serves for the greater purpose and I believe that he has heard with his ears, and he understands with his heart as to what God's purpose is for him. I can wholeheartedly say that Inky has ignited the flame even more for me to continue to serve Jesus and recognize him in all I do because he is the driving force behind what it is I feel that I was called to do.

This next statement is on my own account and I believe that most if not everyone will agree with me when I say that no one is perfect. We all fall short of perfection and we all make mistakes. But as said before, by the power of grace through Jesus we are made right with God, and when Jesus states, "Man shall not live on bread alone, but by every word that comes from the mouth of God," I believe Jesus is saying that we must always keep our eyes on him in all we do. And if we do this, we will live within the Spirit that God so readily gives to the ones that desire to live for his Son.[76] And by living according to the Spirit, we set our minds on the things of the Spirit. And even though we are not perfect, sin will have no dominion over us, since we are not under law but under grace.[77] And it is by grace that we are forgiven.

As a result, by living in the Spirit, understanding with our hearts, and having the blessing of living under grace, we can live by every word that comes from the mouth of God, which I believe Paul readily states for us in Rom 12, *Marks of the True Christian*. I do hope you reference this powerful chapter and I believe this can be summed up by what Paul states in the letter of 1 Corinthians, which says, "So now faith, hope, and love abide, these three; but the greatest of these is love."[78] This is what Jesus so desired from us, that we live through and for him and that we love one another, just as he loved us.[79]

By striving to live by this lesson that Jesus gives us, I also believe that he is challenging us to be great through him. He is challenging us not to just live on bread alone. He is challenging us to take the first step, to seek him out with all our hearts, and to plant the grain of mustard seed. After all, Jesus said that if you have faith like a grain of mustard seed, you can move mountains, and nothing will be impossible for you (please reference back to Matt 17). Jesus stated, "I am the vine; you are the branches. Whoever abides in me and I in him, he it is that bears much fruit, for apart from me you can do nothing."[80] Jesus has presented to us that he is the Way to true clarity and prosperity in life, but he is also being very strict. During his ministry, he sent out his disciples and many others to preach the good news, saying, "The harvest is plentiful, but the laborers are few."[81] He said that if "they receive you, eat what is set before you. . . . But whenever you enter a town and they do not receive you, go into its streets and say, 'Even the dust of your town that clings to our feet we wipe off against you.'"[82] I believe Jesus is essentially saying that his arms are wide open and he will always receive you when you run to him, but he is signifying that once we commit and want to live for him, we will be nothing without him, as I can wholeheartedly say that my outlook and perspective on life has completely changed since I proudly found and decided to follow Jesus and it is something that I would never let go. Even thinking about something such as letting him go is worse than death.

He is also telling those who would accept his words to truly understand them and to follow him like a child. This is what Jesus means when he states multiple times, "For he who has ears to hear, let him hear." His word will remain for us, but it is up to us to accept it and write it on the tablet of our hearts.

As I previously just pointed out, Jesus stressed to us that apart from him we can do nothing. I believe we can relate this to his next temptation after he committed to God. When the enemy promised Jesus riches and glory if he were to fall down and worship him, Jesus said, "Be gone Satan! For it is written, 'You shall worship the Lord your God and him only you shall serve.'"[83] With what I have pointed out thus far, it seems clear that if we desire to be a branch from the vine that is Jesus, and if we continue to have faith like a grain of mustard seed while giving him all the praise and glory through all we do by serving him, we will experience a more bountiful and fruitful life, as I and hopefully you can attest to as well.

If we worship, praise, and give him all the glory through our serving as it relates to what Jesus said in Matt 4:10, then more will be added to us. He so readily makes this known to us by the parable of the sower. While teaching to many people, he said,

> A sower went out to sow. And as he sowed, some seeds fell along the path, and birds came and devoured them. Other seed fell on rocky ground, and given the seed did not have much depth of soil, they immediately sprang up. But when the sun rose, they were scorched, because they had no roots. Other seed fell among thorns, and the thorns grew up and choked it, and it yielded no grain. And other seeds fell into good soil and produced grain, some a hundred-fold, some sixty, and some thirty. He who has ears, let him hear.[84]

After his disciples asked him as to why he speaks in parables, Jesus then stated, "For the one who has, more will be given, and he will have an abundance, but from the one who has not, even what he has will be taken away."[85]

Within the parable of the sower, Jesus is stressing to us that by committing to him, we must have roots within our faith and be able to endure tough times when they do come. By doing so, we will be able to effectively lead and coach in the good times and the bad. Any coach can lead when times are going well, but it takes a great coach to lead in times of a storm or unfruitful season. It is evident that as Christians, we will endure tough times at some point along our coaching path. But if we live by every word that comes from the mouth of God, then we will understand with our heart and trust Jesus when he says, "I am the true vine, and my Father is the vinedresser. Every branch in me that does not bear fruit he takes away, and every branch that does bear fruit he prunes, that it may bear more fruit."[86] Jesus said these things to us because in him, we will have peace in the midst of tribulation.[87] But through our sufferings we may rejoice, "knowing that suffering produces endurance, and endurance produces character, and character produces hope, and hope does not put us to shame."[88] As coaches in Christ, if we have hope and stay faithful in the midst of storms, we will not be shaken because our foundation is steadfast, stable, and faithful.

I believe if we remain true to all of this, then it will be easier for us to decide how to live when storms try to push us away from Jesus. While in the wilderness, the enemy challenged Jesus to throw himself down from the pinnacle of the temple. But Jesus said to him, "Again it is written, 'You shall not put the Lord your God to the test.'"[89] Now again, I am not perfect. None of us are. I have fallen into temptation in my life. Most of us, if not all of us have as well. There have been times in my life when I have gotten it right, but there have been more times when I have gotten it wrong. But these experiences I have had thus far have molded me into the man I desire to be and they have strengthened my faith because they have always redirected me back to my rock and foundation. I believe that as Christians, if we learn from our mistakes and understand with our hearts on how we can utilize them to help us grow, we may bear more fruit if we continue to abide in Jesus, because he will always abide in us if we accept him with all our heart. As he said, "Remain in me, and I will remain in you."[90]

But we must understand what is also written. "No one who abides in him keeps on sinning; no one who keeps on sinning has either seen him or known him. . . . No one born of God makes a practice of sinning, for God's seed abides in him; and he cannot keep on sinning, because he has been born of God."[91] As I've said, we are not perfect and we will never be perfect. But I believe if we learn from our mistakes and utilize them to help us grow as men and women of faith, we can be better coaches of influence throughout our personal testimony and coaching path.

We all can believe this to be true because within the parable of the lost coin in Luke 15, Jesus says,

> Or what woman, having ten silver coins, if she loses one coin, does not light a lamp and sweep the house and seek diligently until she finds it? And when she has found it, she calls together her friends and neighbors, saying, "Rejoice with me, for I have found the coin that I had lost." Just so, I tell you, there is joy before the angels of God over one sinner who repents.[92]

If we learn from our mistakes, understand with our hearts on how they can help us grow as men and women of Jesus, and not commit those transgressions again, angels will minister to us because we did not steer from our foundation. We must continue to lift our eyes to the hills. In this life, as coaches in Christ, we will experience ups, downs, temptations, and fruitfulness. But if we plant our faith in good soil, nothing will completely take us off course. We must continue to run the race with endurance and learn from our mistakes to become better members of Christ. If we are able to do this, we will also become better Christian coaches of influence.

8—Your Inner Circle

As we further progress as coaches in Christ through our ever-developing commitment to Jesus, I believe we must also adopt key attributes to build off the foundational elements of setting him as our rock and committing to him. As we progress through Jesus' ministry, we can see that after he committed to God and after he defeated the temptation of the devil in the wilderness, he then proceeded to surround himself around people that would be a benefit to him. As you know, these people were his twelve disciples. I believe that this is a staple coaching point from Jesus because he is showing us that as we run our race, we must surround ourselves around a team that will help keep us going. In addition, I believe our team should also help us improve at what it is we were ultimately called to do and help us achieve our goals for our greater purpose as coaches in Christ.

We will call our team our inner circle and I believe they should exhibit the three qualities described above. I want us to discuss each quality, how it related to Jesus and his ministry, and how we can utilize them to help us prosper in our future endeavors. But as coaches in Christ, we have set our foundation and we understand who it is we ultimately run this race for. Within our coaching path and within our journey, our inner circle needs to surround our core, our rock and foundation that will never move. He will always be the most important member of our team (as we will discuss his importance within our inner circle multiple times throughout this chapter). Given that we have our base and strong roots that have been planted in good soil, we are now able to build up by surrounding ourselves around people that can help us become better at what we were called to do. As Jesus is the only one who can help us produce good fruits because he is our roots, I believe our inner circle greatly helps us along the way as well. As it is written in the book of Ecclesiastes, "Two are better than one, because they have a good reward for their toil. For if they fall, one will lift up his fellow. . . . Again, if two lie together, they keep warm, but how can one keep warm alone? And though a man might prevail against one who is alone, two will withstand him—a threefold cord is not quickly broken."[93] God also said at the beginning of time in the book of Genesis, "It is not good that the man should be alone; I will make him a helper fit for him."[94] God then proceeded to put a deep sleep over Adam before taking one of his ribs to create Eve, his wife.

Also, while Jesus was on the cross for us, he saw his mother, Mary, and the lone disciple that stood by him on Calvary, John. "When Jesus saw his mother and the disciple whom he loved standing nearby, he said to his mother, 'Woman, behold, your son!' Then he said to the disciple, 'Behold, your mother!' And from that hour the disciple took her to his own home."[95] Even though Jesus would be temporarily leaving them soon, he told John to keep Mary within his inner circle and to hold fast to her because he will soon be with his Father in heaven.

Jesus wants us to have an inner circle to help us grow, but throughout his ministry, he has demonstrated that he must be our roots and we must continue to follow him daily as coaches in Christ. By this foundation, Jesus will lead us to where he wants us to go so we can fulfill our purpose through him. As it is written, "The heart of man plans his way, but the LORD establishes his steps."[96] In time, he will also guide us to people he wants in our lives to help fulfill our purpose. It is by faith that we trust in this, as we already know that "faith is the substance of things hoped for, the evidence of things not seen."[97] It is by these verses and actions of Jesus that we can trust in. Even though there are other examples, we can see that we should also surround ourselves around people that we can trust and that will help us grow as individuals.

But I want to reiterate who are roots are, where our seed is planted, and who our foundation is. Jesus' promise, his peace, and his steadfast love for us is what really matters. He is our driving purpose in life. In the end, if one person or if multiple people are no longer a part of your circle, you know who your foundation is. That rock that you stand on will never crumble and it will never be shaken.

Even though Jesus had thousands of followers during his ministry, we know that he had disciples (also called apostles) that were extremely close to him. It is these disciples whom Jesus trusted throughout his ministry. They were with him when he performed his incredible miracles, and he even discussed the secrets of heaven with them by further explaining the parables of which he spoke in. This ultimately helped him spread the good news because they preached his word to thousands after his time on earth. This directly relates to an important quality of your inner circle, which is that they should help you achieve your purpose and goals. And we know that this was Jesus' purpose because he said,

> For I have come down from heaven, not to do my own will but the will of him who sent me. And this is the will of him who sent me, that I should lose nothing of all that he has given me, but raise it up on the last day. For this is the will of my Father, that everyone who looks on the Son and believes in him should have eternal life, and I will raise him up on the last day.[98]

His apostles helped Jesus because they created disciples of all nations (please refer back to Matt 28:19–20) and they helped further achieve God's will for him by saving more lives through baptisms. It is clear that Jesus' inner circle played a big role in his time on earth, and it is something that we should live by as coaches in Christ so we can continually grow.

As I have previously discussed in the book thus far, my parents have played an immense role in my life. They have been with me through thick and thin and they have agreed with me and stood by my side even when I am wrong. They have taught me so many lessons in my life that I utilize every day. One of those lessons directly relates to our inner circle and what I have described thus far. My parents have told me that throughout your life, the number of people you can truly trust and the ones who will help you grow throughout your life will equate to the five fingers on your hand. It is these five people within your inner circle that you may find trust and comfort. Along with providing trust and comfort in both fruitful and difficult times, I believe you should be able to look to your inner circle for advice and/or guidance in similar times as well.

Now please keep in mind that your inner circle does not have to add up to five people nor does it have to be limited to five either. For example, if your circle includes eight total people such as your two children, your brother and sister, your wife/husband, your parents, and your best friend, that's fantastic! Shoot, Jesus had twelve people in his circle. But with this statement we must also consider who we let into our inner circle. Jesus did have twelve disciples, but we know that one of them, Judas Iscariot, betrayed him, which ultimately led to Jesus' crucifixion. Now by no means am I saying that Jesus, the Son of God, made some sort of mistake. He knew exactly what he was doing. Jesus knew that Judas went away and conversed with the chief priests and officers on how he might betray him and give him over to them in exchange for money. During the Lord's Supper, Jesus said as they were eating,

> "Truly, truly, I say to you, one of you will betray me." . . . so Simon Peter motioned to him to ask Jesus of whom he was speaking. . . . Jesus answered, "It is he to whom I will give this morsel of bread when I have dipped it." So when he had dipped the morsel, he gave it to Judas, the son of Simon Iscariot. . . . Jesus said to him, "What you are going to do, do quickly." . . . Some thought that, because Judas had the moneybag, Jesus was telling him, "Buy what we need for the feast," or that he should give something to the poor. So, after receiving the morsel of bread, he immediately went out. And it was night.[99]

As I previously said, Jesus utilized Judas Iscariot to ultimately fulfill his purpose for us. Jesus knew that he was going to betray him, as you can see from the Scriptures above. But I wanted to utilize this example to express that we should be cautious as to whom we let into our circle. I know there are many people who thought they know someone and trusted them, but were ultimately betrayed. Finding your inner circle takes time and patience and we should be diligent in finding who we can trust and look to for advice. As it is written, "Keep your heart with all vigilance, for from it flow the springs of life."[100] This is why I love my parents' five-finger rule regarding our inner circle. In this day in age, it is hard to find people you can trust and lean on for advice. But if we continue to stand on the rock that holds us together and trust in his purpose and plan for us, we will always continue to strive forward. Now that we have learned a few things about the inner circle according to Jesus and some guidelines associated with it, we are able to dive a little bit deeper into the qualities that your inner circle should possess, how it related to Jesus and his ministry, and how we can utilize the qualities to help us prosper.

Keep You Going

As previously mentioned, I believe the first quality your inner circle should display is that they help keep you moving forward throughout your journey. In addition to our foundation that is Jesus Christ, our inner circle should be our driving force behind what it is we do. We all have goals and we all have things that we want to get better at. Whether that is improving at being a better parent or sibling, a better manager, or wanting to be a strength coach at the highest level, we all need someone to lean on in times of need and we all need people to keep pushing us forward to achieve our goals. I can personally attest to this as I have greatly leaned on two people in my inner circle that mean the most to me in my life, my parents. There have been times in my journey thus far when I have had to deal with things that have been a lot tougher than me. But if I didn't have Jesus as my rock and my parents within my inner circle, those things that were a lot tougher than me would have most likely kept me down and beaten me until I couldn't stand back up. But you know what, with my foundation and inner circle being the driving force behind what it is I do, I always got back up and I always will get back up. That's the beauty in coaching and being mentors to others in the Jesus' name! We are always able to continually get back up when things temporarily knock us down and we can show resiliency beyond the human being's wildest dreams. People will be astounded at your resiliency and resolve in unfruitful seasons and they will wonder and ask how you are able to bear through the tough times. It is because you have your inner circle and your foundation that is Jesus. Not only will this allow you to continually get back up and keep going, but it will resonate amongst others and you will indirectly coach others in a positive way without you being aware of it. I humbly say that this has happened to me before. I have previously been approached by a coach and he asked me about how I can get up and continually go day after day. Even though I was slightly surprised by the question, I told him about my inner circle and my foundation that is Jesus Christ who keeps pushing me forward every day. Now this coach was not a Christian and he didn't know much about Jesus. But just from my simple answer and briefly telling him about my driving force, he wanted to learn more about Jesus and follow him. One thing I did learn that day is you never know who you could influence. Even though you may not realize it, you never know whose life you could positively affect just by your actions. Not only should your inner circle keep you going, but you may positively influence others along the way because of it.

To reiterate, the first quality of our inner circle is paramount if we want to continue to run our race with endurance. Our inner circle should sustain us throughout our journey and should be our rock throughout our life. After Peter (which sounds like "rock" in Greek) confessed Jesus as the Son of God, Jesus said, "And I tell you, you are Peter, and on the rock I will build my church, and the gates of hell shall not prevail against it."[101] Jesus then proceeded to tell his disciples that he must suffer many things, and then be delivered up to the chief priests and elders to be killed, and on the third day be raised. Jesus was utilizing his inner circle to keep his gospel going after his time on earth was to be finished. He set Peter (formerly named Simon) as his rock to help create disciples of all nations. This is apparent in the book of Acts when Peter preached to and saved thousands through baptisms at Pentecost. This is also evident after Peter and John were arrested because they were teaching the word. But many of the people that heard the good news from Peter and John believed in it, and that number came to about five thousand.[102]

In addition, Peter is the author of the letters of 1 and 2 Peter, which reiterate to us to stay strong in our faith while reminding us of the example that Jesus showed. I also want to mention the book of Revelation, which was written by the apostle John. Within the book of Revelation, Jesus appeared to John at the island of Patmos after his resurrection, where he told the apostle to write what he sees in a book and send it to the seven churches.[103] These letters and this book demonstrate how we should act, what we should do in certain circumstances, and what must take place before Jesus returns. Jesus gives us comfort and reassurance within this book by stating multiple times, "I am coming soon."[104] Jesus reiterated to us to follow his word in Rev 21 by saying, "'Behold, I am making all things new.' Also he said, 'Write this down, for these words are trustworthy and true.' And he said to me, 'It is done! I am the Alpha and the Omega, the beginning and the end. To the thirsty I will give from the spring of life without payment. The one who conquers will have this heritage, and I will be his God and he will be my son.'"[105]

I wanted to mention these verses for two reasons. 1) They show that Jesus is the Man and it is these words that provide us comfort and reassurance that we will be with him and he is always with us. 2) Jesus used a member of his inner circle, John (one of his twelve disciples), to write down the words he spoke and this would ultimately become one of the books that we as Christians lean on and trust in with all our hearts.

John played a big role in keeping Jesus' word going. We can also use this example to live by, which is to find people that we can trust in to keep us going, no matter what our circumstance. Now, I also must mention someone who has written much of the letters within the New Testament. This man, Paul, was brutally beaten, afflicted, and persecuted for many years as he traveled far and wide to spread the word of Jesus. We can see throughout the book of Acts that Paul (formerly named Saul) was convicted, arrested, stoned, and held before the council while spreading the word of Christ. Paul traveled to various places including Rome, Corinth, Athens, Thessalonica, Philippi, Ephesus, and Greece to spread the Gospel of Jesus. This ultimately led to his imprisonment, which led him to write some of the various "letters" in the New Testament while in prison (such as the books of Ephesians, Philippians, and Colossians).

For those who are unfamiliar, I would like to mention who Paul was and how he came to being a part of Jesus' inner circle. As previously mentioned, Paul used to be named Saul before he dedicated his life to being a servant of Jesus. He was one of the many who despised Christians after Jesus ascended into heaven. He openly approved of the executions of followers of Jesus (see Acts 7 [the stoning of Stephen] through 8:1–3), and breathed threats and murders against the disciples of the Lord.[106] This led him on a journey to Damascus to attempt to find men and women who served Jesus, that he may bound them and bring them back to Jerusalem. But it was then when a sudden light appeared around him. "And falling to the ground he heard a voice saying to him, 'Saul, Saul, why are you persecuting Me?' And he said, 'Who are you, Lord?' And he said, 'I am Jesus, whom you are persecuting. But rise and enter the city, and you will be told what you are to do.'"[107] Astonishingly, Paul was struck blind by the light that reigned down from heaven! Jesus then proceeded to tell a man named Ananias through a vision that he will go find a man named Saul and lay his hands on him, that his sight may be regained. Ananias was afraid, because he knew that Saul was a persecutor of Christians. "But the Lord said to him, 'Go, for he is a chosen instrument of mine to carry my name before the Gentiles and kings and the children of Israel.'"[108] Once Ananias traveled to the street called Straight, he entered the house of Judas (according to Jesus' command), and he spoke to Saul and laid his hands on him, and "something like scales fell from his eyes, and he regained his sight. Then he rose and was baptized . . . and proclaimed Jesus in the synagogues, saying, 'He is the Son of God.'"[109] (Also, during Paul's time of proclaiming the name of Jesus, he wrote the first letter to the Corinthians while in Ephesus, which includes the verse that the second part of this book is centered upon, which is 1 Cor 9:24).

I wanted to provide some background information about Jesus' inner circle to show you how he operated when choosing his disciples. Also, who knows, maybe this information is new to you and it opened your eyes to how awesome our God is!

From looking at the example of Paul, as well as the other disciples, one would most likely be confused as to why Jesus chose these men to carry out his word and "keep him going." Paul was formerly a persecutor of Christians and openly approved executions of them. While Peter and John did not commit these specific acts, these three men all had one thing in common, and that was to spread the good news of Jesus Christ, even if it was in exchange for their life. For example, Paul testified to the facts about Jesus in Jerusalem against the council, risking his life while the Jews plotted to kill him. But it was through his letters that he wrote that has helped save millions of people's lives to this day by writing most of the New Testament, which has caused people to read them, hear them, and believe in the word.

Please keep in mind that I am only mentioning three members of Jesus' inner circle. However, we can relate these events to his whole inner circle because they were all willing to give their lives to spread the gospel after Jesus ascended into heaven. This previous statement of "they were willing to give their lives for Jesus" brings a great point. I am not saying that every member of your inner circle must be willing to give their life for you, but it is an important quality that we must pay attention to. Willing to give your life for someone is the ultimate form of love, as Jesus said, "This is my commandment, that you love one another as I have loved you. Greater love has no one than this, that someone lay down his life for his friends."[110] Jesus is saying that we must love one another as he loved us, and he demonstrated the ultimate form of love for us. Most of the time, if you have someone as a part of your inner circle, you are most likely a part of theirs as well. There are people in my inner circle that I would most definitely give my life for. We should realize that Jesus gave his life for all of mankind and his inner circle died for him and his word (after he revealed himself to them following his resurrection). This displays the ultimate form of love and trust. For example, if you have a spouse or best friend that would give their life for you, you'd better believe that they will give you everything they have to keep you going in tough times.

As a coach in Christ, I believe what Jesus said to his disciples in the verses directly above (endnote 110) has a very deep and profound meaning. It goes beyond what people typically think of when they think of a coach. Having a passion for something that you are willing to die for displays a completely different level of effort. It displays a completely different level of trust and dedication to what you are committed to. What is your passion? If you're a parent, is it your kids and you want to be the best mentor and coach for them? If you're a spouse, is it your significant other and you want to be able to give the best advice to them when they need it? Or maybe your passion is what you know you were called to do as a coach and you are coaching for the greater purpose, for Jesus Christ. Whatever your coaching path is, we can all learn from the details that Jesus displayed to us throughout his life.

In addition, I would like to reiterate and refer to the other commonality that Jesus' inner circle demonstrated, and that is that they were all very successful people. Jesus' inner circle reached thousands upon thousands of people, proclaiming the gospel to many nations. They demonstrated patience and endurance to help Jesus keep his word going after he called them to make disciples of all nations. But we must also recognize that his disciples were not perfect. In fact, Jesus' inner circle was composed of sinners. Jesus even said, "For I came not to call the righteous, but sinners."[111] Even Peter, whom Jesus classified as his rock (see endnote 101), denied Jesus three times after he was arrested. However, we know that Jesus already knew that Peter would deny him. He said to Peter, "Truly, I tell you, this very night, before the rooster crows, you will deny me three times."[112] (Jesus said this to Peter on the night he was arrested.) And sure enough, this statement from the Son of Man came true. After Peter denied knowing Jesus for the third time, the rooster crowed. "And the Lord turned and looked at Peter. And Peter remembered the saying of the Lord, how he had said to him, 'Before the rooster crows today, you will deny me three times.' And he went out and wept bitterly."[113] Peter felt horrible for what he did and what happened, but again, Jesus knew that this would happen. He told Peter, "Simon, Simon, behold, Satan demanded to have you, that he might sift you like wheat, but I have prayed for you that your faith may not fail. And when you have turned again, strengthen your brothers."[114] It is clear that Peter turned and did strengthen his brothers. In fact, as previously mentioned in this book, it is reported that Peter felt so unworthy to be associated with Jesus, that he wanted to be crucified upside-down (for spreading his gospel) because he didn't deserve to die in the same manner as him. It is clear that Peter wasn't perfect, but he was extremely successful within his mission, which was to spread the name of Jesus to thousands upon thousands of people no matter what the circumstance.

What we can take away from your inner circle thus far is that they should be able to keep you going through many different aspects and situations. And from the events and examples given, we can determine that your inner circle does not have to be composed of perfect people, but they should help you and they should have the desire to see you succeed as hills and valleys are presented to you throughout your life. Paul by no means was perfect, as that is clear through the information given. But he devoted himself to helping Jesus when he called him on the path to Damascus. Finding your inner circle may take a lifetime, but it will pay off when you are able to find people that support you and your desired endeavors with all their heart. In addition, if you can find some members within your inner circle that will be with you through thick and thin, and you both show love to each other that may even go to the point of death (because "greater love has no one than this, that someone lay down his life for his friends" [John 15:13]), you, my friend, have found someone that you should never let go of.

Improve You at What You Were Called to Do

In addition to the first quality that our inner circle should exhibit along with its details, I believe your circle should also improve you at what it is you were ultimately called to do as a coach. Whether that be a parent, a teacher, an older sibling, a sports coach, or a strength coach, we can always learn and get better at what we do. If you're an educator, you can always learn more about the subject or subjects that you teach. If you're a small business owner who is struggling to reach your target market about your product, you can reach out to your inner circle about improving your marketing tactics in hopes that they can get you down the right path. If you're a sports or strength coach such as myself, you can always learn new ways and methodologies to enhance performance within your athletes. Given that I am a strength/performance coach, I could talk about the physiology, biomechanics, and functional anatomy of the body all day. The first thing you probably think of when you think of a strength coach is muscle. And your brain works very similar to skeletal muscle. For example, if you're a running back and you prepared all off-season to get faster and you ended up accomplishing your goals by improving your sprint mechanics and forty-yard-dash time from the enhanced recruitment of your central nervous system and increased muscle mass in your lower half which allowed you to apply more force into the ground, you would probably be jacked up from your improvements! But let's then say you had the mindset to not lift weights throughout the whole in-season (which is an unwise and horrible decision), you would start to lose your muscle mass, which decreases your power output and effectiveness on the field.

Your brain works the same exact way. If you stop lifting weights during the in-season, you're going to become less effective from the loss of muscle mass. Whatever it is you do as a coach, if you don't use your brain to continuously learn and get better at what you do to help improve the ones around you, then you will become stale and less effective. I also believe you must first invest in and create happiness within yourself before you can have a true, positive, and meaningful impact on others.

I am able to say that I am fortunate enough to have people within my inner circle that I can call not only to keep me going, but they can also help improve me as a strength coach. This is a blessing because it is rare to find people that will show loyalty to you not just as a coach, but as a human being.

As a coach, we are all educators, and it is our duty as coaches in Christ to give everything we have to it (this statement will be displayed more in Part III through our servant mindset). Times always change and there is always room for improvement at what we do. If we are able to get just a little bit better at our craft every day, our effectiveness towards others will be immense. I am not saying that you need to call someone within your inner circle every day and ask for advice on how you can improve. Depending on the status of your relationship with that person, you may obviously come off as an annoyance. But seeking to get better through various methods and having the ability to call someone within your inner circle to seek their advice on the matter can go a long way in our development as coaches.

For example, I always look to get better by researching new methods within the sports performance industry and applying them with my athletes. I am then able to call someone that I really know and trust to get their opinion on the method and see how they would implement it or how they would put a "spin" on it. By this, I mean that they may take part of the new method and implement it with their current ideologies towards training to make it even better. This not only sparks great conversation, but it causes both of us to grow as sports performance coaches. This can relate to any occupation that has a direct impact on other people. For example, if you're a professor or teacher that presents new research findings to your colleague that possibly debunks your current teachings to your students, then this may initiate great conversation amongst yourselves and can challenge you to get better as an educator to learn more. By learning more and continually seeking to progress from the help of your inner circle, this will directly relate to the effectiveness that you have towards those whom you coach.

I hope you can take this example and utilize it to who you are as a coach. Are you a motivational speaker, a teacher, a parent, a CEO of a company, or a mentor towards a young group of kids in an after-school program? I challenge you to take these principles and how it related to Jesus' life and incorporate it into your life. I hope you can conceptually apply some of these principles thus far and mold them into your coaching path. After all, we are all different and we all have a different testimony to share. By this challenge, we are now able to go into Jesus' ministry and I want to show you, to the best of my ability, how he challenged his disciples to be great and how this methodology should relate to your inner circle in which they challenge you to be great as well. After all, in addition to Jesus' goal of showing us the way through his example of humbling himself and becoming obedient to the point of death on a cross for us (see Phil 2:8), he was able to improve the effectiveness of his disciples so they were ultimately able to proclaim the gospel to many nations after his time on earth.

To start, I would like to exhibit challenges from our rock and foundation, the Man whom our inner circle ultimately stands on. Earlier, I alluded to our inner circle standing on our rock that is Jesus, and if one member of our circle departs due to a multitude of possible reasons, we as coaches in Christ will never fall because our base is built on the solid foundation of life and truth. He is obviously the backbone of our inner circle, which has been displayed throughout the book thus far. In addition to him challenging his disciples, he challenges us directly in many ways. I wanted to point out key things that stick out in my mind and things that Jesus said which drive me to get better every day at what I do.

The first example I want to talk about takes us to the birth of Jesus, as I would like to describe some of his challenges to us in chronological order according to his life. I would first like us to note where Jesus was born. We know that Joseph initially wanted to divorce Mary in a quiet and just manner because she was found to be pregnant before they came together after being married. "But as he considered this things, behold, an angel of the Lord appeared to him in a dream, saying, 'Joseph, son of David, do not fear to take Mary as your wife, for that which is conceived in her is from the Holy Spirit. She will bear a son, and you shall call his name Jesus, for he will save his people from their sins.'"[115] While they were in Bethlehem,

Mary "gave birth to her firstborn son and wrapped him in swaddling cloths and laid him in a manger, because there was no place for them in the inn."[116]

As we read through the Gospels in their entirety, we can look back and see that Jesus challenged us to be great from the very beginning. Jesus, the Son of God, was not born in a palace and he was surely not welcomed by some people of authority (see Matt 2 for King Herod's reaction to Jesus' birth). God in the flesh was born in a manger, in swaddled cloths, at a less opportune place compared to an inn. The humility in Jesus' birth says it all. As we examine Jesus' ministry by reading through the Gospels all the way through his ascension into heaven, we can see that God is telling us that big things can come from small beginnings, and I firmly believe that. Jesus Christ, the Son of God, came to earth to show us the way as he became the most influential Man to ever live. He wants us to seek improvement, and he wants you to be great with him, together. For he has said, "With man this is impossible, but with God all things are possible."[117] Jesus wants to be the primary member of your inner circle. He wants to take on the challenges with you so you can improve and continually run the race in such a way to get the prize.

Jesus, from being born in a manger in the small town of Bethlehem to growing up in Nazareth, demonstrated to us that we all have the ability to be great, no matter where we are from or what our background is. Even as Jesus was starting his ministry and began to call his disciples, people were saying, "Can anything good come out of Nazareth?"[118] Jesus then spoke of previous events to Nathaniel that already occurred in his life, leaving him astounded. Jesus then said to him, "Truly, truly, I say to you, you will see heaven opened, and the angels of God ascending and descending on the Son of Man."[119] In other words, Jesus is saying, "Man, you thought that was good, boy you haven't seen nothin' yet."

When Jesus began his ministry, he was very determined in his approach. Everything he said and did related to success. To give another example, in the book of Mark, after Jesus called his disciples and healed many, he began to preach in Galilee. As many people were looking for him, he said, "Let us go on to the next towns, that I may preach there also, for that is why I came out."[120] Jesus continued his determination by healing many people and preaching in many places. He taught and gave the most influential speech in the history of mankind (cf. the Sermon on the Mount, Matt 5). This was all in the midst of being ridiculed by many people, and the chief priests and scribes wanted him killed because he was a threat to them and their authority.

Despite the presence of rejection and criticism from his works at times, he kept going. While he taught in his hometown of Nazareth, many heard him and were astonished. They questioned him by saying things like, "'Where did this man get these things? What is the wisdom given to him? Isn't this the carpenter, the son of Mary and brother of James and Joses and Judas and Simon?'" Jesus marveled at their unbelief, but he went about among the villages and continued to teach.[121] Through Jesus' example, despite the doubt, he kept going. He did not quit. He wanted to show to his disciples and to us that in the midst of adversity, he kept moving forward. He maintained strict persistence in pursuit of his goals. Greatness was his only option.

Not only did he maintain his persistence and show that greatness is his only option, but he did it by bringing others with him. Jesus explained the secrets of the kingdom of heaven to his disciples, he taught them how to live, and he performed his miracles in the presence of them (i.e., calming a storm, healing many, feeding of the four thousand, and walking on water). Jesus told them, "Heal the sick, raise the dead, cleanse lepers, cast out demons. You received without paying; give without pay."[122] Jesus wanted them to take his teachings and continue to heal and spread the good news. Jesus told them, "If anyone will not receive you or listen to your words, shake off the dust from your feet when you leave that house or town."[123] He then encouraged them to maintain their persistence and strength by saying, "Behold, I am sending you out in the midst of wolves, so be wise as serpents and innocent as doves."[124] Jesus challenged them to be great, with faith being their stronghold and their rock.

From the example of persistence that Jesus continually demonstrated, there are key takeaways that we can utilize from the above example as coaches in Christ. I first mentioned that Jesus performed many of his miracles in the presence of his disciples. I want to refer to the specific miracles that I mentioned, and then describe the scenario behind them so we can utilize them in our own lives as coaches to positively influence others.

Obviously, I am not saying that you need to physically calm a storm, walk on water, or feed four thousand people with seven loaves of bread and a few small fish. That clearly would be impossible. But what I am saying is we as coaches in Christ can be a positive influence, or in some cases a miracle, for those whom we coach if we can utilize some of the concepts behind some of his miracles.

I am not attempting to take his miracles and messages behind them out of context. Throughout all his miracles, there is a message behind them and he is showing us that he is the answer to the problem. And through these messages, I believe we can attempt to mimic the characteristics that Jesus displayed and utilize the meaning behind what he said so we can have a profound impact on others. Jesus wants us to lead like him and live for him. Jesus is our miracle. When he calmed the storm in the presence of his disciples, Jesus is showing us that in the midst of every storm, he will be our peace and he will give us rest. Within Jesus' miracles, he provided an incredible answer to a problem that was present, and given that he is the primary member within our inner circle, we can greatly improve at what we do as coaches in Christ.

I would like to refer to the miracle that I briefly mentioned, in which he calmed a storm in the presence of his disciples. As it is written in the Gospels, his disciples were greatly stressed and anxious when the storm was present. They did not know what to do or where to go. Jesus, on the other hand, was calm, cool, and collected. He was actually asleep in the back on a cushion! When his disciples woke him up because of their fear, Jesus simply awoke and rebuked the winds, leaving them stunned. "And he said to them, 'Why are you afraid, O you of little faith?' Then he rose and rebuked the winds and the sea, and there was a great calm."[125]

Jesus, being the leader of his disciples, demonstrated an amazing quality that we can learn from, which is leading and approaching a problem in a state of calmness. If we attempt to solve a problem in the state of panic and frustration, an effective solution will most likely not be met and we will probably enter a downward spiral of more frustration and impatience. We will not be able to succeed as a leader if we exhibit frustration and impatience in the midst of a problem. (As coaches, we can all attest and agree with this).

As a leader, people will look up to you. They will mimic the characteristics that you exhibit and the results you get from those whom you coach will coincide with how effective you are as a leader/coach. If you are able to exhibit a state of calmness in the presence of problems, that mentality will radiate to those whom you coach because you are setting a standard. If you habitually demonstrate calmness if problems arise, the solution will come much easier and efficiency will be the result.

Now as a coach in Christ, our state of peace and our state of calmness comes from Jesus. We lift our eyes to him in order to bring peace to help solve a solution. But with every problem that is present, we must remember that we have to physically take action in order to solve it. My parents always told me, "God will give you the oars, but you have to row the boat." He will most definitely help row the boat with us, but we must go out and find the solution if adversity hits. This directly relates to what I described earlier of when Jesus sent out his disciples after teaching them his principles and standards. He told them that he is sending them out in the midst of wolves and to shake off the dust and move on if someone does not accept you. In essence, God gave them the oars, and he wants them to go out and row the boat. If we can improve on our calmness in the presence of storms or problems, our effectiveness as a leader will improve because not only will this result in more efficiency, but this state of calmness in certain situations will manifest to others and in turn can help positively influence their decision making in the presence of adversity.

The next example that we can learn from Jesus as we continue this race is how he acted when he performed his miracles. Again, please don't take what I'm saying out of context. As said previously, Jesus wants us to lead like him, so we are able to ultimately glorify his name through what we do. Jesus performed a variety of healings such that he healed the blind, he enabled the deaf to hear, and he allowed paralytics to walk by simply laying his hands on them. We obviously cannot do that. But what we can do is go deeper into the context and see that Jesus had an immensely positive impact on their lives. I believe we can lead like Jesus if we adopt the qualities and persona that he presented during these healings so it can equate to having a positive impact on other people's lives. As a precaution and warning, please know that I am not a doctor and the advice that I am giving does not relate to anyone that may have mental, emotional, physical, or any issues that need attention. If you need to see a professional or a doctor, go get help. What I am saying is that we can utilize the characteristics that Jesus exhibited to provide guidance to someone that is looking to get back on track or get better at what they do, whether that be an athlete looking for help to get better, a student who is looking to you for help so they can get an A on their final exam, or any circumstance in which someone is looking to you as their coach for help. After all, Jesus told us, "Give to the one who begs from you, and do not refuse the one who would borrow from you."[126] I hope you are able to use some of the characteristics that Jesus exhibited during his healings and conceptually apply it to who you are as a coach so you can have a positive impact on others.

I believe there are three main qualities that Jesus demonstrated while he performed his healings. One could substitute or add different qualities and characteristics in certain instances, but we can see that in almost every case, Jesus showed the characteristics of humility, servitude, and compassion. (The characteristics of humility and servitude will be discussed in detail in part III.) I would now like to give some examples from Scripture and explain how we can apply these to our lives.

Within Matt 8, Mark 1, and Luke 5, Jesus performed the miracle of healing a leper. During this event, we can see that this man begged and pleaded to Jesus to heal him. Scripture tells us that Jesus showed much pity towards the man. He showed compassion towards this man because he desperately needed help. After Jesus touched him, the man was made clean, and Jesus told him not to tell anyone that he healed him, but to go and show himself to the priest and make an offering for his cleansing. Within this example, we can see that Jesus demonstrated all three qualities, which resulted in him clearly having a positive impact on this man's life.

We can relate this example to one similar in which Jesus healed two blind men in Matt 9. In a similar manner, these two men cried out, "Son of David, have mercy on us!" Jesus proceeded to touch their eyes because of their belief, and their eyes were opened. After this, he told them to tell no one, further demonstrating his humility.

By referring to Matt 9, in which Jesus heals two blind men, we can see that at the beginning of this passage that Jesus came to these men after he already performed the miraculous healing of raising a girl back to life.

This event took place in which a ruler knelt before him, pleading for his help to raise his daughter back to life. Jesus then followed him and after the journey to the ruler's house, he saw the great crowd that had assembled to pay respect for her death. Jesus then said, "'Go away, for the girl is not dead but sleeping.' And they laughed at him."[127] However, when he told the crowd to go outside, he took the girl by the hand, and she got up and arose. Jesus then strictly charged them to tell no one about this (refer to Mark 5:43 and Luke 8:56).

In addition to the qualities mentioned above, we can see that Jesus is also showing a characteristic that we as coaches can benefit from, and that is making sure that we do not neglect people that need our help the most. I believe the Gospels are trying to tell us this because after Jesus said that she is only sleeping, the crowd behind him laughed, yet he still performed a miracle and had a positive impact not only on the young girl, but on her father because Jesus raised her up. As a coach, he achieved a miracle when no one else thought it was possible.

There will be times within our life when someone will undoubtedly say, "Don't worry about him/her, they aren't that important." Whether you're a teacher, manager, CEO, or a team leader, we should all see value in someone and we should all be able to utilize that value in some capacity to encourage and inspire. This can relate to you being a teacher and taking that extra time to help one of your students who asks of your assistance, as he/she wants to "prove his/her colleagues wrong" by getting an A on that final exam. Or, this can relate to your daughter who wants to make the high school basketball team and she asks her dad for extra help because the coaches at school say her jump shot isn't good enough right now. Or, maybe you are a manager or CEO of a business and you decided to delegate a task to a shy person that had the specific strengths needed that no one else saw, leaving the other colleagues laughing and stunned, while the other employee finally felt the empowerment he/she has been looking for which positively changed their mentality towards other aspects of life.

I believe the key takeaway from this message is that Jesus took the girl by the hand and she walked. As coaches, we need to be able to take that person by the hand, raise them up, and help them through times of need when we are called upon as coaches. Even though it won't always result in the desired outcome for that individual, we as coaches are responsible for showing a standard of excellence and coaching certain characteristics in that person's mind so it will have a positive effect in their future. Characteristics such as resiliency, resolve, and a passion for what they want to accomplish so he/she can apply these qualities to achieve their goals now and in the future.

Even though these are only a few of the many healings that Jesus performed during his ministry, as previously stated, they all seem to refer to the presentation of humility, servitude, and compassion while also directly relating to resiliency and resolve in certain cases. For us to continually improve as coaches in Christ, I believe we must first invest in ourselves by always trying to get better at our craft while also making sure we are happy within the process. Within this section, I spoke of improving ourselves first (through our inner circle challenging us to be great in addition to taking the time to improve and invest in ourselves) because of its primary importance.

If you question this judgement, you may ask yourself, "How can you value other people and try to make everyone else around you happy if you don't first value yourself by doing what makes you happy or taking care of your priorities?" In some instances, before Jesus performed his miracles, he withdrew to desolate places to pray because he needed to take care of his priorities first (we will talk about this more in the next chapter).

If we first have the commitment of investing within ourselves to get better at our craft while also making sure we are happy throughout the process, we can then utilize Jesus' coaching tips for improvement to the best of our ability. We are then able to continually improve upon and coach others with the mindset of maintaining humility and servitude while demonstrating true compassion towards others. "For the LORD sees not as man sees: man looks on the outward appearance, but the LORD looks on the heart."[128] By investing in ourselves and making sure we are happy deep within our heart, then others will truly see our compassion towards them when they need our help because it will be real and true. If we don't develop this within ourselves, not only will it be hard to sustain trusted relationships, but it will be hard to maintain the quality of humility while demonstrating the act of servitude. We need to truly value and take care of ourselves so the other qualities of improvement can have true meaning and purpose behind them. And most importantly, we must maintain our identity through the process as brothers and sisters in Christ. Jesus was able to maintain humility and compassion towards others because he had a driving purpose behind his mission and he held fast to his identity, our God. If we plant the mustard seed with the qualities of valuing ourselves and making sure we are happy, in addition to demonstrating humility, servitude, and true compassion towards others while maintaining our identity that is Jesus, our improvements as coaches in Christ will be able to move mountains.

Help to Accomplish Your Goals

The last quality of importance that your inner circle should possess equates to the addition of our previous two. Meaning that if your inner circle keeps you going and they challenge you to be great, your goals will be able to be accomplished. I say this with affirmation because it entails the deepest and most important quality that Jesus demonstrated, and that is love. Our inner circle should be our driving force as coaches in Christ, because they are the driving force behind what we do.

I want to describe this quality in such a way that relates to you, in which that by your new or current determination towards accomplishing your goals, you will radiate that mindset of determination and drive towards who it is you are a coach for. As previously described, we need to make sure that we as coaches have true determination within ourselves first, before we can successfully be a mentor towards others. I say this affirmation also because Jesus found his inner determination and purpose first from God. As previously mentioned within the book thus far, we can see that before Jesus performed some of his greatest miracles, he withdrew to desolate places to pray. And before Judas, his betrayer, and the chief priests arrested him in the garden of Gethsemane to ultimately be crucified, he prayed deeply. He prayed so deeply for his driving force to give him strength. Jesus was so distraught and troubled that he began to sweat drops of blood. The enemy and the temptation tried to keep Jesus away from accomplishing his goal, but he refused. One of the last things he said in prayer before being arrested was "My Father, if it be possible, let this cup pass from me; nevertheless, not as I, but as you will."[129] Jesus was so determined because he was going to succeed in accomplishing his goal because of his love for us. Jesus didn't take no for an answer. His only option was success. And he was able to achieve this success because of his driving force, God. For Jesus said, "I can do nothing on my own. As I hear, I judge, and my judgement is just, because I seek not my own will but the will of him who sent me."[130] In addition, while speaking to the Pharisees, we can see in Scripture that Jesus said, "When you have lifted up the Son of Man, then you will know that I am he, and that I do nothing on my own authority, but speak just as the Father taught me. And he who sent me is with me. He has not left me alone, for I always do the things that are pleasing to him."[131]

As you know, God's will for Jesus was the driving force behind his ministry. Jesus' driving force was so great, that he had an indescribable love and passion within himself. This relates back to the beginning of the book when I gave the definition of "Passion." Jesus reinvented the meaning of this word by the love he showed for us and the determination towards his destiny. His only option was to accomplish his goal, which was to be the Savior of the world by being crucified for our transgressions and conquering death. And from the previous verses given from Scripture, we can see that his driving force, God, was the reason for his triumph.

We needed to first talk about Jesus' driving force and the characteristic he displayed within that determination to accomplish his goals so we can understand what it means to have a nonperishable strength, willpower, and fortitude towards achieving our goals. With Jesus as our driving force with the combination of indescribable love for him, nothing will be impossible for you.

Inky Johnson, who I have previously mentioned, is able to articulate the purpose and driving force behind what he does with an amazing sense of fire and passion during his speeches. If you do not know who Inky Johnson is, you must look him up. Whether it be on YouTube or on his website, www.inkyjohnson.com, he will positively change the way you see life and he will inspire you to settle for nothing less than greatness. He has changed the way I go about life on a day-to-day basis, and I know he will have a positive effect on you.

The key thing that stands out to me when I hear Inky speak is that he stresses that life is a blessing and a gift and our goals should not just be about us. It's bigger than us. Our goals should be about continuing to go for our driving force and leaving a positive effect on other people. He said that as you go throughout life, you will find a challenge or obstacle in front of you that's a lot bigger and tougher than you, and if you don't have a driving force and a reason behind what you do, you'll give up every time. I wanted to mention Inky because he gives affirmation that we need our reason, our purpose, and our driving force always burning inside us if we want to be great. This will lead me into my next topic, which is how we can see and continuously approach life.

As coaches in Christ, if we want to be great at what we do, there will be times when we have to go through something hard. There will be times when we will have to show great courage in taking that next step in order to keep progressing, even if that means it's a temporary step backwards.

I picture our lives as Christians as a staircase. The very bottom is who we used to be before we fully committed our lives to Jesus, for I would like to relate our bottom step to a verse that Paul wrote to the churches around Ephesus, which states, "to put off your old self, which belongs to your former manner of life and is corrupt through deceitful desires, and to be renewed in the spirit of your minds, and to put on the new self, created after the likeness of God in true righteousness and holiness."[132]

I wanted to have this verse as our bottom step because prior to having Jesus in our lives, our sin was in vain. By believing, we are forgiven and we can learn from it for the greater purpose because we are under grace. Shoot, I mess up every day and I am the farthest from perfect, but I try to learn from things that I really botch up on and I try to remind myself who my foundation is. In addition, once he is the center of our lives, we are certainly made new, in which we are placed on a new staircase that is for the greater purpose. Our bottom step is who we used to be before we had a different level of burning passion within ourselves to be great. Having this verse as the bottom step will always remind us to never fall away from who we now belong to and it always reminds us who we run this race for. There will obviously be times in life when things try to take you off that path, things that may push you down a few steps (I can absolutely attest to this and I'm probably raising my hand higher than most from this statement). But given that Christ's level of passion can reign within you, your only option is to get up, to keep going, and to achieve your goals to honor him.

As your journey continues through your new level of determination, you will begin to take leaps and bounds up towards your goals because of a new drive that burns in your heart that is eternal. As you strive up, this can be synonymous with a verse that has been mentioned previously in this book, Matt 17:20. As we begin to strive up mentally and spiritually from our bottom step, we have firmly planted the mustard seed that is our faith within our foundational soil, Jesus. Jesus utilizes a mustard seed because it is one of the smallest seeds, and ends up becoming the largest tree within the garden. I believe this can relate back to the second section of this chapter when I stated that Jesus challenged us to be great from the very beginning, when he was born in a manager, in a more inopportune place compared to an inn because there wasn't room for him, in the small town of Bethlehem. The mustard seed is of the smallest seeds, and this is where we all start. But by planting it within our foundational soil, we will ultimately grow into the twenty-to-thirty-foot-tall tree that also spreads twenty feet wide. As we begin our journey with our driving force keeping us going along the way, we will certainly achieve measurable goals as time proceeds. I say this with affirmation because goal achievement is directly correlated with your level of determination. Whether you say you can or you can't, you are right. And as time proceeds, your faith (that is the mustard seed) will continue to grow. This will directly affect your level of determination, resiliency, and resolve towards certain situations. I say this from personal experience because I have hit things in my life thus far that have been a lot tougher than me. And if I didn't have the driving force and the purpose for what I do, I would have given up in those situations, but I didn't. I kept going.

The beautiful thing about the parable of the mustard seed is that as we grow through our spirituality, mentality, and mindset, there will be times when we run into those things that are a lot tougher than us. There will be times when we want to stop or quit. There will be times when God puts us into situations where we think he may not be with us, but ultimately, he puts us into those situations so we become more dependent on him. He puts us into tough situations not to harm us, but he does this to mold us into who he wants us to become. He does this to make a stronger version of ourselves, so we are able to withstand any obstacle that is in front of us. In other words, he is pruning us into who he wants us to be.

If we hit something in life that seems to push us one step back, know that it is only temporary. With Jesus on your team, you will always win. Always. Whether it is something temporary you have been fighting, or if you feel like you haven't seen the light of day for a long time, please know that you are his. Jesus said in the book of John, "My sheep hear my voice, and I know them, and they follow me. I give them eternal life, and they will never perish, and no one will snatch them out of my hand."[133] He has put you through difficult times because he knows you can handle it. He has put that heavy weight on your back because he knows you will stand it back up. But with that weight, he is wanting to strengthen that level of determination and resiliency within your foundational roots. He will help you, but he wants you to take that first step. He will give us the oars and will help row the boat, but he is wanting us to initiate that first step for our passion that is Jesus that reigns inside us.

This leads me into a verse we can lean on if it seems that we have taken the temporary step backwards, which is John 15:1–2. Within these verses, Jesus said, "I am the true vine, and my Father is the vinedresser. Every branch in me that does not bear fruit he takes away, and every branch that does bear fruit he prunes, that it may bear more fruit." The vinedresser prunes because he is wanting the tree to develop a strong structure that will result in a more desirable form for the future. And by God pruning us, we will ultimately bear more fruit and become stronger men and women of faith as coaches in Christ. And with us becoming stronger individuals, those previous obstacles will be no match for the person that God is molding you to become.

And as time proceeds and as we become the man or woman of faith that God wants us to be, the small mustard seed that we used to be will turn into the largest tree in the garden. As we continue to relate our journey upward to the parable of the mustard seed, we must look at how Jesus ends this amazing parable. Jesus said that as we become a tree, the birds of the air will come and make nests in our branches. (You can reference the parable of the mustard seed in Matt 13, Mark 4, and Luke 13)

This is how we become effective coaches in Christ. Once we have planted ourselves in our foundational roots and have grown both spiritually and mentally, we who used to be that tiny mustard seed will have grown into one of the largest trees in the garden which people can lean on for guidance. I believe the birds of the air are those for whom we are a coach, whether it be your athletes, your employees, your children, or anyone that you have influence on. And they will be able to make their nests in the shade that you provide.[134]

I hope that you can see from my past experiences in Part I and throughout the book thus far that I am a living testimony to what I have written. Everyone has their own testimony and it is my hope that you can relate your coaching path and your life to what I have written within this chapter. As coaches in Christ, it is imperative that we always continue this journey, we never get off this staircase, and we never quit on the race of life that we are running. I believe that requires guidance and advice from our foundational roots, Jesus. Our next chapter will relate to how Jesus sought out advice from his foundational roots, God, and how we must always seek guidance from our brother so we always stay on course.

9—Guidance through Prayer

As we continue upon our staircase and as we continue to run this race of life, I believe we must take into account a key coaching point from Jesus as to how he sought out advice, and that is through constant prayer. Within this chapter, I want to discuss the context behind what I believe Jesus is trying to teach us when he went to pray to the best of my ability, and how we can then learn from this and apply it to our lives.

I wanted to discuss this topic immediately following our discussion of the parable of the mustard seed because in addition to overcoming obstacles and challenges within our coaching path, prayer is what strengthens our faith and it is what allows the mustard seed to grow. Jesus said in Matt 17:20 that "if we have faith like a grain of mustard seed, we will be able to move mountains." And once that seed is planted in the foundational soil of Christ, we will begin to grow and then be pruned periodically by the vinedresser (God), which will result in us growing even stronger upwards as he is molding us into the strongest version of ourselves.

Experiences and learning from them for the greater purpose will certainly allow the mustard seed to grow, but throughout Jesus' ministry, we can see that he was strengthened through prayer. I believe this is one of Jesus' greatest and most important coaching points to us as we continue to run this race to get the prize. By planting our mustard seed and committing to the foundational soil of Jesus, I believe prayer is what ultimately causes our roots to grow.

Reading the parables that Jesus spoke in and connecting the dots within his ministry is so incredible. Jesus' roots were made stronger and they were made deeper through prayer. As previously mentioned, Jesus prayed so deeply in the garden of Gethsemane on the night he was arrested. He prayed so deeply that within this time, he began to sweat drops of blood (as noted, a condition termed "hematidrosis"). Jesus could have given up, but he sought out guidance and comfort from God to keep going. During this time, he said, "'Father, if You are willing, remove this cup from me. Nevertheless, not my will, but yours, be done.' And there appeared to him an angel from heaven, strengthening him."[135] We can see that Jesus was praying to God at a time when he desperately needed him. But the angel that appeared to him strengthened his foundational roots to keep going so he would accomplish his goal of saving us from our sin so we may have life in heaven by believing in him. After withdrawing to a desolate place to pray in Gethsemane, he proceeded to walk back to his disciples (who were sleeping) after going to pray three times. As Jesus told them that the hour had come for him to be betrayed, Judas and a crowd that was composed of chief priests, scribes, and elders had appeared in the garden to take him. Jesus openly accepted his destiny by walking back to his disciples to be betrayed by Judas, as Jesus knew that the crowd of betrayers would be there. His roots were strengthened within his foundational soil that is our Father, and he knew he could take on his destiny. Jesus knew that he could embrace the winds and storm that was in front of him, and it was because he continually sought out guidance and comfort from God throughout his life, which allowed his roots to grow so deep and strong that he could take on anything, having come down from heaven to show us the way.

From the example above, on the night Jesus was arrested, we can see he prayed so deeply to God at a time when he needed his strength. Jesus prayed in a time of need. And throughout the Gospels, it is clear that Jesus prayed to God in multiple situations.

We can now turn to Mark 1:35, which reads, "And rising very early in the morning, while it was still dark, he departed and went out to a desolate place, and there he prayed." And after his disciples searched and found him, they said that everyone was looking for him. Jesus proceeded to say, "Let us go on to the next towns, that I may preach there also, for that is why I came out." We can see from this example that Jesus didn't just pray to God in times of need, he prayed to him in the morning, before he started his day. And to paraphrase, Jesus then proceeded to tell his disciples, "Let's go conquer the day."

As coaches in Christ, I believe this is a critical coaching point from Jesus. He is demonstrating to us that we should always start our day with God. Just like how we should water a plant and its roots every day for it to maintain its health and for it to grow, we should do our best to start our day with God so we can grow. Prayer is the water for the mustard seed that is our faith. Praying in times of need will most certainly allow our roots to grow in our foundational soil and God will never forsake his children. But we must consider that it is not the only time we should pray. Jesus also demonstrated that he wants us to start the day with him through prayer. He wants us to realize that he will be that protection for us in times of need and desperation, and Jesus is also telling us that he wants to be a part of our journey every day and he wants to conquer each day with us.

In addition to Jesus starting his day with God and also praying in times of need, we can now turn to Luke 6:12–13, which reads, "In these days He went out to the mountain to pray, and all night He continued in prayer to God. And when day came, he called his disciples and chose from them twelve." I believe this is a scenario that we can most definitely learn from in which it states that Jesus continued in prayer to God and he was doing it at a different time as compared to the morning. Jesus didn't just pray in times of need and he didn't just start his day with God, he continued in prayer with him throughout the night.

Now, we know that Jesus was perfect. He was the Man that was without sin, who served the ultimate penalty for us. In every aspect of his life, he was perfect. If Jesus is telling us that we have to pray all night until the sun comes up, I will be the first one to tell you that I am failing miserably at it. I bet all of us would be failing miserably at it. But what I do believe he is telling us when he prayed all through the night is that God must be our priority. He has made this known to us in John 15, when he states, "I am the vine; you are the branches. Whoever abides in me and I in him, he it is that bears much fruit, for apart from me you can do nothing" (please refer back to John 15:5).

I believe we can also refer this back to Jesus' parable of the mustard seed because if we have abided and firmly planted ourselves within our foundational soil, the only way we can grow for the greater purpose is through Jesus. No seed can grow without water and soil, and as we have previously pointed out, prayer is the water that helps our roots grow and our foundational soil is Jesus. If we continue to water our mustard seed every day, our roots will grow stronger, which will result in a greater integrity and steadfastness to what we hold onto and believe in as coaches in Christ.

From these two examples, we can now travel to a different scenario in which Jesus prayed within his ministry. We will look to Matt 14, when he performed the miracle of feeding the five thousand. There are multiple things we can take away from this event; however, I want to focus on certain things Jesus did so we may learn from them.

(Please follow along with me in Matt 14:13–23. You can also reference the feeding of the five thousand in Mark 6, Luke 9, and John 6.) In the feeding of the five thousand, many people

> followed him on foot from the towns. When he went ashore he saw a great crowd, and he had compassion on them and healed their sick. Now when it was evening, the disciples came to him and said, "This is a desolate place, and the day is now over; send the crowds away to go into the villages and buy food for themselves." But Jesus said, "They need not go away; you give them something to eat." They said to him, "We have only five loaves here and two fish." And he said, "Bring them here to me." Then he ordered the crowds to sit down on the grass, and taking the five loaves and two fish, he looked up to heaven and said a blessing. Then he broke the loaves and gave them to the disciples, and the disciples gave them to the crowds. And they all ate and were satisfied. And they took up twelve baskets full of the broken pieces left over. . . .
> Immediately he made the disciples get into the boat and go before him to the other side, while he dismissed the crowds. And after he had dismissed the crowds, he went up on the mountain by himself to pray.[136]

After Jesus performed this miracle, we can see that he then proceeded to go up to the mountain to be alone to pray. Throughout all the times that Jesus prayed, I believe we can learn something from them. As compared to when Jesus prayed to God in the garden of Gethsemane in a time of need, here we can see that Jesus went to pray after an amazing and beautiful moment. As coaches in Christ, I believe Jesus is telling us that we will strengthen our relationship and deepen our roots within him if we pray in the best of times, and in the most difficult times. Jesus wants to be a part of our lives during every moment. He wants to be a part of the joy when things go right. He wants to be a part of the championship, the promotion, the acceptance letter into college, the day your child is born, or any day that brings joy to your heart. He also wants to be with you in times of grief, sadness, and pain, in which we know this is to make us stronger. For if we reference back to Eccl 3:1–3, we know that "for everything there is a season, and a time for every matter under Heaven, including a time to pluck up what has been planted, a time to break down, and a time to build up." This is to ultimately make us stronger through what Jesus told us in John 15 by first pruning us before we are built up.

Even though there are a myriad of other examples of when Jesus prayed, we can see from the examples above that he prayed to God in four completely different spectrums. He prayed in a time of desperation and need, he started his day with God by praying in the morning, he continued in prayer with God at night, and he also prayed to God after great accomplishments. I believe this is a critical coaching point and lesson that Jesus is demonstrating to us as we continue to run the race that is our life and coaching journey. He wants to be the shelter we run to in times of desperation and need and he wants to be a part of our ups and downs that ultimately lead to our success. We must go through some valleys if we want to stand on the mountain, and this is something that I have continued to learn and grow from as my life progresses. Those valleys that you have previously been in or are currently in are not there to harm you. We know that God is using those valleys to build us into the strongest version of ourselves. And he is using those learning experiences to prosper us and give us hope and a future, not to harm us (please reference back to Jer 29:11). To quote Inky Johnson again, "The things that happen to us in life were not designed to stop us. They're designed to reposition us so we can come in contact for what God really has for us."

Based on these four different spectrums as to when Jesus prayed (in need, in the morning, throughout the night, and in times of joy), we can see that God was Jesus' priority. He prayed in a myriad of different situations so his roots would grow deeper. His roots were so deep, that even after our Lord was cut down, he was able to come back as the strongest tree this world will ever see, as he was able to rebuild his temple after just three days.

If we only pray in certain times (i.e., times of need), our roots will only grow so deep. But if we make Jesus our priority and develop a deeper relationship with him by also praying in times of joy and by walking with him throughout our day, we will add another dimension to the growth of our mustard seed. By praying in different aspects of our life, this will not only help our roots grow deeper, but these added dimensions will allow our roots to grow stronger and thicker. Having roots that are deep, strong, and thick within our foundational soil will result in the growth of a bigger and more expanded tree, which will ultimately allow the birds of the air (who we are a coach for) to have greater shade. And we know as coaches in Christ that this is our number one goal, to have a positive influence on others and to provide the greatest impact we can. If our roots are firmly established through what has been described thus far, I believe that from our experiences, we can have a greater impact on others by our guidance to them. And this is from our maturity and strength to get through past situations, which led us to become better versions of ourselves.

From this, we should take into account one more critical coaching point from Jesus while he was in prayer. Throughout the examples given, and through the myriad of times that Jesus prayed, we should note where he went to pray. In the garden of Gethsemane, he was with Peter, James, and John, but he told them to remain where they were at, for he went farther within the garden by himself, to pray. And as we read in Mark 1:35, in the morning before his disciples went searching for him, Jesus went out by himself to a desolate place to pray. We can also see that in Luke 6:12–13 when Jesus prayed throughout the night, he did so out by himself, out on the mountain. This is similar to the last scenario we spoke of, when Jesus fed the five thousand. After this amazing event, "immediately he made the disciples get into the boat and go before him to the other side, while he dismissed the crowds. And after he had dismissed the crowds, he went up on the mountain by himself to pray. When evening came, he was there alone."[137]

We can see that throughout all these scenarios, Jesus went to a desolate place to pray, by himself. Please note that this is not limited to just these four examples. As we read through the Gospels, we can see that every time Jesus prayed, he went to a desolate place so he could be in prayer with God alone. This critical coaching point from Jesus signifies that while in deep prayer, we should be away from the noises, away from the distractions, and away from the chaos. Just you and him. For it is written, "But when you pray, go into your room and shut the door and pray to your Father who is in secret. And your Father who sees in secret will reward you."[138]

I wanted to point out this coaching point within Scripture, but not in a way as if it were a strict rule. The beautiful thing about Christianity is that we do not live under a standard of rules. We live under grace for what Jesus did for us. For as it is written in the letter to the Romans, "because, if you confess with your mouth that Jesus is Lord and believe in your heart that God raised Him from the dead, you will be saved."[139] And most importantly, we know this is true because Jesus stated, "For God so loved the world, that He gave His only Son, that whoever believes in Him should not perish but have eternal life" (please reference back to John 3:16). If you find it in your heart that you and a group of other people want to pray in public, that's fantastic! Or if your athletes and yourself want to pray in the end zone while the crowd is roaring during pregame, that's great too. Or if there is any situation where you find it in your heart to pray with someone that is not in complete solitude, that's perfectly fine. For Jesus said, "For where two or three are gathered in my name, there am I among them."[140] For Jesus is always with us wherever we call upon him.

But I wanted to point out that Jesus continually prayed in solitude because I believe that's where he truly deepened his relationship with his Father. While praying in solitude, it's just you and him. No one else. This is where you can be yourself. You can express what has truly been on your mind and what you have been thinking about. Whether that results in tears of sadness, tears of joy, or if you want to pray about something that you want to keep between you and him.

For being in solitude is where we can develop a true, deep, and genuine relationship with God. He wants us to be in solitude with him. He wants us to cast all our burdens on him so he can guide us and lift us up through the comfort he provides. For it is written, "Cast your burden on the LORD, and he will sustain you; he will never permit the righteous to be moved."[141] In addition, Peter, Jesus' rock in which he built his church, said, "Cast all your anxiety on him because he cares for you."[142]

Also, Paul, as we know was formerly named Saul, openly accepted and encouraged the death of Christians until Jesus revealed his majesty to Saul while he was walking on a path to Damascus, in which Saul then committed his life to Jesus, risking his life multiple times while proceeding to write a majority of the letters within the New Testament. (For more information about this event, please reference to Acts 9. You can also turn back to chapter 8 of this book, in which we discuss this event in the section, "Keep you going.") And within the letter to the Philippians, Paul stated, "Do not be anxious about anything, but in everything by prayer and supplication with thanksgiving let your requests be made known to God."[143]

I wanted to express this verse within Philippians and reference back to whom Paul formerly was because it doesn't matter who you formerly were or what was in your past. God cares about who you are right now. Once Jesus is our priority and we recognize him as the Good Shepherd, we will become one of his sheep. For he told us, "Truly, truly, I say to you, I am the door of the sheep. . . . I am the good shepherd. The good shepherd lays down his life for the sheep. . . . I know my own and my own know me. . . .

My sheep hear my voice, and I know them, and they follow me. . . . I give them eternal life and they will never perish, and no one will snatch them out of my hand."[144]

Jesus doesn't care how broken you think your past may have been or the sin you've committed in the past (myself included). He wants us to strive towards the future with him, while learning from our past mistakes and becoming more ingrained and dependent on our faith, so we may recognize our past and see how far we've come as more mature individuals and coaches in Christ. Paul confirms this through his testimony by saying, "Brothers, I do not consider that I have made it my own. But one thing I do: forgetting what lies behind and straining forward to what lies ahead, I press on toward the goal for the prize of the upward call of God in Christ Jesus."[145] As you can see, Paul does state that we should forget what lies behind; however, we should note that Paul still recognized his past. For in the letter to the Galatians, he said, "For you have heard of my former life in Judaism, how I persecuted the church of God violently and tried to destroy it. And I was advancing in Judaism beyond many of my own age among my people, so extremely zealous was I for the traditions of my fathers. But when he who had set me apart before I was born, and who called me by his grace, was pleased to reveal his Son to me, in order that I might preach him among the Gentiles, I did not immediately consult with anyone."[146]

As you can see from the Scripture above that is written in the Psalms, 1 Peter, and Philippians, that Jesus wants us to cast all our burdens on him. And as we begin to learn more about Paul and his past, we know that God wants to turn our past transgressions into our ultimate triumph. He called all of us to be one body in Christ. He even called Paul, the most unlikely person who openly reviled Christianity, to carry on his word throughout multiple nations and to write much of the New Testament.

As we read deeper into the above Scripture from Paul, we can see that he was extremely "open" to us by expressing his past, as he does multiple times throughout Scripture and his testimony. And as we read through the letters within the New Testament, Paul states what he/we will become through faith in Christ. Within the letter to the Romans, Paul states, "For I consider that the sufferings of this present time are not worth comparing with the glory that is to be revealed to us."[147] I believe we can compare this with what Paul stated within the first letter to the Corinthians, "There are heavenly bodies and earthly bodies, but the glory of the heavenly is of one kind, and the glory of the earthly is of another."[148] Throughout his ministry, he stresses to continually strive forward by living for Jesus and cherishing what will soon be revealed to us. "When Christ who is your life appears, then you also will appear with him in glory."[149]

As you can see, Paul recognizes his past as well as who he will become in the future. For what we strive for on earth does not compare to what is for us in heaven, but God calls us to be great now as well. He wants us to run the race in such a way to get the prize (please reference back to 1 Cor 9:24) and he wants us to move mountains (please reference back to Matt 17:20). He wants us to be the best we can be and that is made possible for us because we can live for something greater, that is his Son.

I also want to point out that I said that Paul recognizes who he "will" become and not who he "wants" to be. Paul was so ingrained and steadfast to what he believed in, that there was no option other than success. For we know that if we believe in Jesus, we will be saved. And through the above Scripture (1 Cor 9:24 and Matt 17:20), God wants us to apply this confidence and hope to our lives on earth as well. For Jesus tells us, "With man it is impossible, but not with God. For all things are possible with God" (please refer to endnote 117).

This leads me into our next point within prayer. Even though God wants us to cast our burdens on him, this is not the only thing he wants from us. For it is written, "Commit your work to the LORD, and your plans will be established."[150] We can plan our way, but it is God who establishes our steps (please refer back to endnote 96). For as described above, if we show confidence and hope within our faith (through the example of Paul) and run in such a way as to get the prize while committing our work to God, we *will* accomplish our goals and move mountains. God knows what you desire, and he wants to accomplish those goals with you by first expressing them to him in prayer.

With God, whether you say you can do something or cannot, you are right. Throughout the book thus far, I hope you can see that Jesus and Paul did not attempt to accomplish their goals for themselves. They had the driving purpose of God to keep them going. As we reference back to Phil 3:13–14, Paul refers to continuing to press on towards the goal for the prize of the upward call of God in Christ Jesus. God calls every single one of us to be great. And as Christian coaches, I believe the Passion that Paul showed to accomplish his goals throughout his ministry can also be unlocked within us once we have Jesus in our hearts. We can truly be great when we have an eternal passion burning inside us. I firmly believe this to be true because I think one can only accomplish his/her true potential when he/she has a deeper meaning for success. If we are only out for ourselves, we can only get so high before we meet something that's a lot tougher than us. We may hit something that relates to breaking us down emotionally, physically, or psychologically. But the mind and spirit is an incredibly hard thing to break, and with the Passion of Jesus ruling in our hearts, we will never be broken. The only thing that is stopping you from accomplishing your goals is the weak side in all of us that tells us to stop. But finding the deeper purpose within us and striving towards the future for Jesus, nothing will be impossible for you. And God wants you to express this to him in prayer. He wants you to be great with him because as we strive forward, he wants us to recognize that he is the Alpha and the Omega and he is the roots to our successes.

Throughout this chapter, it is my hope that I have pointed out to what I believe are critical aspects of prayer for us as we seek out guidance. We first talked about Jesus within his ministry and when he prayed, in which he prayed in the morning, in times of desperation, in times of joy, and he continued in prayer throughout the night with God. In short, Jesus made God his priority and he continued to walk with him at all times.

And within the example of when Jesus prayed in times of desperation, we spoke of the night when he prayed to God in the garden of Gethsemane. Previously within this chapter, I mentioned Scriptures from the Psalms and 1 Peter, which tells us to cast our anxieties on God, because he cares for us and he will never allow his righteous people to be moved. I also mentioned Prov 16:3 and 16:9, which tells us to commit our plans to the Lord, and they will be established. For we plan our way, but it is God who establishes our steps. I ultimately wanted to mention the Scriptures from the Psalms, 1 Peter, and Proverbs because they all relate back to our driving force, Jesus. As we look at the time when Jesus was in the garden of Gethsemane, we can see through his desperation that he clearly casted his anxieties and burdens on God while in prayer (Pss 55:22 and 1 Pet 5:7). In addition, his life's work was centered around commitment to God (Prov 16:3), and nothing was going to stop him, because he had his driving purpose. Nothing was going to hinder him from accomplishing his goal of saving the world from our sin. And as previously discussed, Jesus asked God if he would remove this cup from him (that is, the penalty he was going to face for the sin we committed) in the garden of Gethsemane. But he then said, "Nevertheless, not my will, but yours, be done" (please reference endnote 135). Through Jesus' determination and commitment, he knew what he had to do. There was no doubt that Jesus was going to accomplish his goal, but we know that he accomplished it through the steps that God established for him (Prov 16:9) (i.e., his crucifixion).

We can see that Jesus utilized these key verses that we mentioned while in prayer, and I believe this is something we should learn from. Jesus asked God if he would take the unfathomable pain away that he was going to face. But Jesus knew that it wasn't about him. His life's work was for something greater. His life's work and goal accomplishment was for you, me, and everyone else on this earth, and his driving purpose was God and the process that was set out for him.

In Part I of this book, while explaining my journey, I mentioned that when I was younger, I thought it was about me. I thought that if I truly burned for having Jesus in my heart, I could determine my way in addition to asking him for a Passion that we could conquer together. However, I've learned in time that this is not the case. If you ask Jesus for something that will ultimately reveal his glory through the process, he will give it to you. For he said, "Ask, and it will be given to you; seek, and you will find; knock, and it will be opened to you. For everyone who asks receives, and the one who seeks finds, and to the one who knocks it will be opened."[151] Previously, I used to ask for random things. Things that I just wanted for myself that had no meaning behind them. I don't believe this is what God wants. As we read slowly through Matt 7:7–8, Jesus is telling us to ask for him. He's saying, "If you truly ask for Me, I will bring good things to you."

As I've matured in my life, I've learned that once I put aside asking for silly things, and focused on the bigger picture, things started to unfold for me. When I burned for Jesus and wanted more of him every day, asking him to lay out a plan for us that we may conquer together so people may see his glory and greatness, things started to flow to me (as I hope you saw this in detail in Part I). By things flowing towards me, I mean that doors have opened to me that has allowed me to coach people at various levels, by helping improve athletes' performance through the Passion that Christ gave me. And through his process, God has placed mentors in front of me that have changed my life in a positive way. It is through his Passion that I try to coach my heart out and learn to get better every day. Through my life experiences, I've learned that once we recognize that it is Jesus who we must work for every day, his majesty and presence in your life will continue to grow, as he has in mine. For it is written, "He must increase, but I must decrease. . . . For he whom God has sent utters the words of God, for he gives the Spirit without measure."[152] And as God starts to move more in your life, he will positively affect others through you.

Through Jesus' determination and drive towards serving other people, his Passion radiated towards thousands. And in this case, we have been talking about a man whom Jesus called to continue his word across nations, Paul. Jesus inspired Paul by displaying incredible Passion, love, work ethic, and determination towards the process in which he served, and I believe Jesus wanted us to display these qualities on our journey so it may encourage others to show an increased level of Passion, love, work ethic, and determination as well. As leaders and coaches, it is our duty to bring people up with us, including the people that don't want to be a part of or are distant from the "team." Your team is synonymous and is composed of you and your students, you and your colleagues, you and your employees, or you and your athletes, for example. It is easy to encourage and reach people that are already driven, but I believe that through Jesus calling Paul, he is expressing to us that we must not forget about people that need us most. Paul used to be an extremely stubborn individual that was oblivious to the light, until Jesus reached down and pulled him up. Everybody has an incredible potential within them, and through the drive that currently or hopefully has be opened to you, you may be the leader that starts to unlock that potential through who it is you coach. As previously stated, the mind is an incredibly hard thing to break. By people seeing your Passion and drive towards what you do, as the leader, people will begin to emulate that. And if you have a group of individuals that mimic your mentality and drive, you will help produce a recipe for incredible success, not just in your place of business or on the field, but for these individuals in life. And if someone or a few happen to ask you about Jesus, and you are able to grab them, that's a bonus and a miracle!

Throughout this chapter thus far, we have discussed when Jesus prayed, where he prayed, and what he prayed for. We then discussed events that Jesus encountered and how praying helped him through those experiences. This helped Jesus display his determination and Passion, which resulted in people emulating his determination, work ethic, and drive. It is through our prayer life that will help us continue onward in the best of times and the hardest of times. This will not only deepen our roots within Jesus, but it will help us stay focused and become more ingrained in the qualities of Passion, work ethic, determination, and drive towards goal achievement.

And it is through this consistent action when others will take notice, which can radiate towards others and positively affect them as well.

There is one more thing that I want to discuss as it relates to our personal life in prayer. We know that Jesus consistently went to desolate places to pray so he could be alone with God. In this day in age, desolate places can be hard to come by, but I believe it is a place that we all need to find if we want to truly express ourselves and deepen our relationship with God.

Like anything else, the best work is done in solitude. The greatest champions perform consistent action when no one else is watching. For example, the greatest NBA players take hundreds upon hundreds of jump shots per day in solitude. The best writers write in solitude, the best musicians work on their craft while alone, and the best students continue to study when no one else is watching. And the greatest Champion of all time, Jesus, consistently prayed while in solitude. My question to you is, "Where is your desolate place?"

Personally, for me, this place is my car, where there are no outside distractions, no one can hear me, and I can truly express what is on my mind. My intimate prayer life and relationship with God has increased so much in due large part because of my place of solitude with him. It's just me, God, and the open road. I don't have to worry about anyone bothering me and I can be myself. God wants you to be true when you are in prayer with him, and I believe this is best done in a place of solitude. This is the example that Jesus showed us through his prayer life.

Your desolate place can be anywhere that you feel the most comfortable. It could be your bedroom, your car, or maybe while you are on a walk. It's where you feel the most comfortable to have a conversation with God and it's a place where you can consistently go to. You may have to wait until after school, work, or practice, but you know your desolate place is always there. And this is a place I encourage you to find to help deepen your roots, as it consistently helps me as well.

Thus far, we have discussed critical components to finding the coach within ourselves. We have discussed the establishment of our identity through commitment, our inner circle and its components, as well as the power and guidance of prayer. But like all journeys and all races that we run, we must continue onward when we feel tired, and we must press on toward the goal for the prize of the upward call of God in Christ Jesus for us (please reference endnote 145). Throughout our path and throughout the race we run, we must maintain our driving force.

10—Maintain Our Driving Force

THROUGHOUT MY LIFE THUS far, there is something that I have learned. This is something that is not new and it is not an original idea, but I feel it is something that we often neglect. I hit upon this idea when I mentioned our life being compared to a staircase, in which there will be things in our life that try to push us down a few steps and will challenge us to get back up and climb higher than before. But most importantly, Jesus spoke about this when he told us that he is the vine, we are the branches within him, and God is the vinedresser. As we have previously spoke about, Jesus said that God prunes the branches that bear fruit, so that they may bear more fruit. I wanted to come back to this topic and make it a chapter of its own because I wanted to stress its importance. I believe maintaining our driving force in the midst of adversity creates and unleashes the destiny that God has for us. During our race, our coaching path, and our life, we will experience hard times. We will experience tough times. We will hit things in our life that will attempt to bury us. And they will continue to try and bury us if we don't hold fast to our integrity and what we believe in. I am very fortunate and blessed to have not encountered major catastrophes in my life, but I sure have experienced things thus far that have tried to bury me. And I have experienced things in my life that have tested me. But because of my faith and inner circle, I was able to become a stronger version of myself. As I previously talked about in depth, I believe this is why Jesus surrounded himself around his disciples. This is why he expressed to us that apart from him we can do nothing (see John 15:5). Jesus is telling us that we all need an inner circle, and he needs to be the center of it if we desire to rise to the potential that God has in store for us. He told us that in this life we will have tribulation, but to take heart because he has overcome the world (see John 16:33).

We all have our own testimony and we all have our own story. We will all experience different challenges and difficulties within our life. But by maintaining our driving force and continuing to run our race in such a way as to get the prize, you will climb higher than ever before. Given that we all have different experiences, I want to discuss some of Jesus' relatable coaching points throughout his ministry so that you may apply them to your life during the valleys before you ultimately ascend the mountain through your faith! I believe this is an important topic to discuss because if we hold fast to Jesus' words and live by his coaching points that we will discuss, we will not only rise to another level and become stronger versions of ourselves when adversity hits, but we will become even better coaches because others will envy your mentality and determination to continually run when everything in this world tries to hold you down and tells you to stop. When adversity hits, you'll continue to run towards your goal and you will continue to rise up because you have something greater burning in your heart that no one can take away. Jesus calls us to pray, maintain, and grow our relationship with him (as described last chapter). He calls us to have a burning Passion for him through his example, and he never wants us to lose that fire for him that's in our hearts.

I want to note that we are only discussing a few coaching points and they do not compare to the myriad of amazing examples and coaching points that Jesus demonstrated to us. These coaching points stick out in my mind and are a reminder to me to keep going to not only try and create a stronger version of myself, but that my experiences and my journey may positively impact others in hopes that others see him through me.

The first example I want to give, I believe, signifies that God can use adversity or take something that we think seems so insignificant in our lives, and make it a miracle through us that can positively influence others. I believe this to be true by Jesus' miracle of the feeding of the four thousand. As coaches, we know that our journey and our process isn't just about us. The coaching path we encounter and our life story isn't a linear progression. When challenges or adversity hits, I believe our testimony is about setting an example for others and being remembered for the Man that lives through us. It's about overcoming and conquering to become stronger versions of ourselves to not only realize the true potential that we have inside us through Christ, but that it may have a positive influence on who it is you coach because of the standard you set.

(Please feel free to follow along in Matt 15. You can also reference Mark 8.) To explain the miracle of the feeding of the four thousand, Jesus was first accompanied by his disciples as well as a crowd of approximately four thousand people. He had been with the crowd for three days and was unwilling to send them home hungry.

> And the disciples said to him, "Where are we to get enough bread in such a desolate place to feed so great a crowd?" And Jesus said to them, "How many loaves do you have?" They said, "Seven, and a few small fish." And directing the crowd to sit down on the ground, he took the seven loaves and the fish, and having given thanks he broke them and gave them to the disciples, and the disciples gave them to the crowds. And they all ate and were satisfied. And they took up seven baskets full of the broken pieces left over.[153]

I believe this miracle signifies what we have described thus far and is an example that Jesus can move through our lives to serve as a blessing for others. We mentioned that God can take adversity or something that seems so insignificant to us and turn it into a triumph not just for us, but for others. In the miracle of the feeding of the four thousand, the adversity that is displayed is being in a desolate place with seemingly very little food for over four thousand people. (I believe the breaking of the bread can also be signified as adversity, which we will talk about.) We all experience different loads and levels of adversity, as this miracle can be conceptually applied to situations you have been in or may encounter in the future. The disciples then basically told Jesus that we only have seven loaves of bread and a few fish. How are we to feed such a great crowd with such little food?

Even though Jesus' disciples were confused as to how they were going to feed over four thousand people with such little food, Jesus had other plans. Contrary to the disciples' confusion, Jesus saw this adversity as an opportunity to bless others through someone else. What Jesus proceeds to do next clearly demonstrates that the previous statement is true. Jesus then took the bread, broke it, and then gave it to his disciples. The disciples then proceeded to distribute it to the crowd.

I now want to refer back to when I said that the breaking of the bread can also be viewed as a time of adversity. But not only can it be viewed as a time of adversity within our lives, I believe it can be viewed as a challenge or a tough time that God knows we can overcome. It can be viewed as a situation in which God is placing something before us that he knows we can handle. He is molding us into stronger versions of ourselves. For it is written, "But now, O LORD, you are our Father; we are the clay, and you are our potter; we are all the work of your hand."[154] And God will never place something in front of us that we cannot handle. As it is written, "No temptation has overtaken you that is not common to man. God is faithtful, and he will not let you be tempted beyond your ability, but with the temptation he will also provide the way of escape, that you may be able to endure it."[155] Our temptation is equivalent to giving up, to giving in, or not giving everything we have in order to overcome. When adversity hits or challenges are presented to us, we must flip our thinking from "Why me?" to "Why not me?"

At times, when challenges are presented to us, we can move around it. We can slide by and think that everything is all well and good, but in reality, it's only treating the source of pain and not the root cause. If you keep putting a bag of ice over your knee because it hurts after every time you run, eventually you will have to stop running because of the pain (you give up), or you will have to get surgery because you are completely broken (the challenge will completely overcome you). (As a side note, the root cause of many knee problems from running is either a lack of strength and stability at your hip or mobility at your ankle.) If we don't deal with the root cause of a problem or challenge, not only may you be negatively affected, but others around you may be ill affected as well. As an analogy, if you want to continue to run the race, you have to deal with challenges head on. They will not only make you a stronger person, but overcoming that challenge or phase of adversity can serve as a blessing to others. For example, in the face of adversity, you continually push through when times are tough and you overcome an obstacle that's presented to you. Or, you accomplish something that no one else thinks you can do. By your actions, you are indirectly coaching people by your perseverance, resolve, and resiliency. By overcoming and by accomplishing what you set out to do, you can serve as an inspiration to others so they may achieve their own goals and dreams. My dad tells me something every day that I believe we all can learn from. He tells me, "It's going to be a great day, and it's going to be a better day than yesterday," no matter what the circumstance. If we continue to ask ourselves, "Why not me?" when adversity or challenges hit us instead of "Why me?," our effectiveness to serve as coaches in Christ will be greater than ever before. I believe our escape in the midst of temptation is hitting "obstacles" in front of us head on and treating them as opportunities to build better versions of ourselves because by doing so, we are allowing God to flow through us to assist in his blessings to others because we continue to overcome and conquer adversity for our driving force, Jesus.

After Jesus broke the bread and gave it to his disciples, they then distributed the bread (the blessing) to the crowd. I believe the key takeaway from the feeding of the four thousand is that in hard or confusing times (as they were in a desolate place with very little food), we must be broken before we can receive the blessing. Maintaining our faith in the midst of challenges or adversity I believe is a key component to growth amongst ourselves, and on the other side of the challenges, adversity, or pain we may face is our promise. On the other side of the temporary pain is your blessing. For as we continue reading through this miracle, we read that after the disciples distributed the bread to the crowd "they all ate and were satisfied. And they took up seven baskets full of the broken pieces left over."[156] I believe God is telling us that he can take something so insignificant or he can take a situation in which we think there is no possible way anything good can come out of it, and turn it into an abundant blessing if we trust him and give everything we have for him.

Through this miracle, we have discussed that through hardships, challenges, or adversity, we still have the opportunity to help serve as a blessing to others, whether that be directly or through our example. We have also discussed that by facing challenges or adversity head on, you are able to become a stronger version of yourself and deepen your roots within our foundational soil. So, when even bigger storms come your way, you will not be broken because of the strength your roots have developed.

But in addition to becoming stronger versions of ourselves, I would like to reference back to a statement that I believe is incredibly important when adversity hits us. It is a key statement that we should believe in when challenges are presented to us, and that statement is, "On the other side of your pain, is your promise." I believe the great Sylvester Stallone said it best.

> The world ain't all sunshine and rainbows. It's a very mean and nasty place and I don't care how tough you are, it will beat you to your knees and keep you there permanently if you let it. You, me, or nobody is gonna hit as hard as life. But it ain't about how hard you hit. It's about how hard you can get hit and keep moving forward; how much you can take and keep moving forward. That's how winnin' is done![157]

The next coaching point I want to discuss demonstrates that through Jesus' example, we will all find our promise on the other side of our temporary pain.

Jesus clearly demonstrated this to us on the night he was unnecessarily arrested, beginning in the garden of Gethsemane. In the garden, on the night he was arrested, he made a choice to face the challenge that was in front of him. But he didn't just make a choice to face this challenge, he made the choice to succeed, no matter what it took. He knew he was going to conquer the challenge in front of him because he had God burning in his heart, and with God, anything is possible (please reference endnote 117).

Jesus faced an unfathomable amount of pain for us through the beatings and the scourging in addition to his crucifixion. He faced the ultimate challenge, the ultimate adversity, and the ultimate hardship, for us. And our hero knew that his pain was temporary. After he suffered for us, he received his promise through his resurrection. Jesus set the ultimate example for us as coaches in Christ. He is showing us that if we push through challenges for him and with him, we will receive our promise after the temporary pain we experience. The world continually tried to beat Jesus down on his final walk to his crucifixion site, but he kept moving. He kept going for us and for God. And on the other side of the unfathomable amount of pain he experienced, was his promise. He was crowned the ultimate Champion of the world. Jesus' example to us is demonstrating that we should always maintain our driving force, as he did. But in addition to maintaining his integrity, we can see that he displayed incredible perseverance and determination. And as coaches in Christ, we can see that the qualities of perseverance, determination, and maintaining our driving force will guarantee your success. Because through him, you will come out on top, and you will receive your reward.

The next example I want to give coincides and builds upon our previous example of Jesus' ultimate triumph, conquering and overcoming death for us. It builds upon the example that Jesus maintained his driving force throughout his entire life, which ascended him to his ultimate glory. He maintained his driving force through great times (i.e., through his healings and miracles), incredibly hard times (i.e., the night he was arrested all the way through his crucifixion), and everywhere in between (i.e., maintaining his constant prayer life). Jesus told us directly, "I can do nothing on my own."[158] Jesus was able to exhibit the potential that God had for him because he always had our Father burning in his heart. The example that Jesus demonstrated to us in which we can greatly learn from takes place in the same chapter of John (chapter 5). While speaking, Jesus said, "I do not receive glory from people. . . . How can you believe, when you receive glory from one another and do not seek the glory that comes from the only God?"[159]

In this day in age, it is very easy to get caught up in outside sources that try to pull us away from God. It is very easy for us to lose sight of the bigger purpose. Now, please don't take this the wrong way and think that I am claiming to be some perfect person that never loses focus or never falls into outside sources of this world. I am extremely far from perfect, and I will never come close to it. As said before, I am a sinner that is just looking for the bread that Christ provides to us. There have been times in my life when I have lost focus and I have gotten caught up in other things. But there is something that I will never lose, and that is a Passion for Jesus that I believe we are able to find in the midst of desperation. There is one thing I know for certain, Passion will always trump a temporary loss of focus. And Passion will lead you right back to where you belong, which is living for Christ.

By going for and seeking glory from God, we are able to find true satisfaction, true comfort, and true success through what it is we do, because it's for a purpose that's bigger than ourselves. By having your driving force, you will be able to break through barriers that try to hold you back. We can see this through the example that Jesus demonstrated to us throughout his ministry. He exhibited that his life's work was for his driving force and he did not back down. He was consistent in his approach to spreading the good news, no matter how many things tried to hold him back.

He was even rejected in his hometown of Nazareth. By following along in Mark 6, we can see that Jesus proceeded to come to his hometown with his disciples, and he began to teach in the synagogue. However, people were astonished as they said, "'Where did this man get these things? What is the wisdom given to him? How are such mighty works done by his hands? Is not this the carpenter, the son of Mary and brother of James and Joses and Judas and Simon? And are not his sisters here with us?' And they took offense at him."[160] Jesus could do no mighty works there other than laying his hands on a few sick people and healing them, because of their unbelief. But Jesus, by his consistent action towards greatness, left and "went about among the villages teaching."[161]

Through this example, we can see that God is telling us that people will reject you and people will doubt you. People will question you and people will try to bring you down. But as Mr. Stallone said earlier, "It ain't about how hard you hit, it's about how hard you can get hit and keep moving forward.

How much you can take, and keep moving forward." I believe the only thing that stops you from being great is yourself. I believe greatness is achieved by harnessing and utilizing the qualities that Jesus exhibited through the examples we have given in this chapter. We can see that Jesus demonstrated an immeasurable amount of perseverance and determination towards his ultimate goal. And throughout his ministry, he performed and maintained the consistent action of spreading the good news, no matter what. As you can see in the example above, even though people in his hometown rejected him, he shook off the dust and kept moving forward, despite the criticism.

Through Jesus' coaching points to us, we can see that as coaches in Christ, we must display great levels of perseverance and determination in addition to taking the consistent action needed to unleash success within ourselves. However, if we desire to have the true potential that God wants to unleash within us, the qualities of perseverance, determination, and consistent action must be wrapped in our driving force, Jesus. This is clear when God expresses to us that Jesus is his Son, his chosen One, and to listen to him.[162] As coaches in Christ, we can succeed in anything we put our minds to, if we wrap the necessary qualities within our driving force. I believe this unleashes a true Passion that God wants to reveal within all of us. All we have to do is find it within ourselves to seek him with our whole heart (Jer 29:13), open our eyes, hear with our ears, and turn to him (Matt 13:15).

Within Part II, we have discussed establishing our coaching identity in Christ. We have also talked about having our inner circle with Jesus being the center of it in addition to continually seeking guidance through prayer. Not only will we be able to seek his guidance through prayer, but this will allow our dependency on him to grow, which will result in us being better equipped to maintain our driving force during the storms, adversity, or challenges that may come our way.

I believe the beautiful thing about this is as our dependency on him grows, our perseverance, determination, and desire to maintain consistent action towards our goals linearly progresses with it. This is because we have Passion and purpose for something that's greater than ourselves. And being that this will help us maintain our driving force throughout our life, it will be that much easier to consistently live by God's advice to us, which is what we will discuss in the next chapter.

11—Tablets of a Coach's Heart

As we hold steadfast to our driving force through what it is we do as coaches, I believe we must also hold God's coaching cues close to our hearts as it will allow us to continually grow and prosper as coaches in Christ. I want to provide some of God's coaching cues as they serve as a reinforcement to us to continually go and continually push when it seems like everything in the world tells us to stop. After all, every coach needs his/her own coach to look upon for advice, and who better to look to than God and his word.

I want to provide five of God's coaching cues that I believe serve as a great reminder to us as leaders that we all have the Great I Am to look to and we all are lucky enough to live under his grace. But I also want to provide some of God's coaching cues that remind us that we have the ultimate power on our team, Jesus. But with this power comes great responsibility to others through how we live and coach.

God's word and Jesus' ministry is filled with an unfathomable amount of coaching cues. There is something we can learn on every page within the Bible. But please keep in mind, I am only providing five coaching cues. As I stated in the beginning of this book and as I have previously mentioned, I am not a theologian and I don't have the gift of being able to dissect Jesus' word in such a way that pierces people's hearts in an uplifting way like some pastors do. I just want to be a sheep on the same side of the fence as our Good Shepherd, Jesus.

I believe these coaching cues are not only a great reinforcement, they are a daily reminder that we all have the power to be an incredible leader. By holding fast to these coaching cues, I believe it will set the foundation for Part III of this book, which will allow the newfound coach within us to help better serve others so they can reach their true potential. After all, that is our goal as coaches and that is what Jesus called us to do, which is to serve for God. With that being said, let us now discuss some of these coaching cues that God provides to us, that we may not only live by them, but write them on the tablets of our hearts so we may always remain steadfast to them.

Matt 10:8 "You Received without Paying; Give without Pay."

As we continue our race and coaching journey, we must recognize that we have the ability to develop an ever-growing Passion for God that he wants to instill within us, and that is by coaching every day for his Son and our King, Jesus. All we have to do is turn to him (please reference back to Matt 13:15) every day and recognize that he needs to be our priority. Once we recognize him as our priority, then our dependency on him will grow. And as our dependency on him grows, our faith will linearly progress with it. As we become more ingrained within our faith and as our roots become stronger within our foundational soil, the Spirit inside us will grow deeper. I believe this is what Jesus wants us to open our eyes to when he states, "Ask, and it will be given to you, seek, and you will find; knock, and it will be opened to you. For everyone who asks receives and the one who seeks finds, and to the one who knocks it will be opened" (refer to endnote 151).

I believe Jesus is saying that as the Spirit inside us grows deeper as a result of the maturity of our faith, we will continue to magnify what we have been seeking, which is a Passion for Jesus that I believe leads to the enduring determination, perseverance, and consistent action we previously spoke about because it is for someone who is so much greater than us.

With all this being said, I believe it can be boiled down to one simple variable, and that is by truly asking Jesus into our hearts. By truly asking him into our heart, we will want him to be our priority, which I believe in turn will cause our dependency on him to grow. As a result, our faith will grow deeper and his Spirit will live inside us, which will allow us to succeed as a coach for him because of the perseverance, determination, and consistent action taken because he is our driving force. Once we truly seek him with all we have and ask him into our lives, the rest will follow if we put in the work, and you will succeed because he will be right next to you every step of the way as your Helper. For he told us after his resurrection and before he ascended into heaven, "And behold, I am with you always, to the end of the age."[163]

Jesus' Spirit is something that is given to us. It is not something we earn. It is something we find by asking and seeking with all our heart. This is what God wants from us. He wants us to recognize that he is the Alpha and the Omega and our path to life. And as sinful as we are, he still wants to show his unmeasurable and insurmountable love for us. God was brutally crucified on a cross for us, to save us from death and to show us how much he loves us. Even while he had stakes being driven through his body on the cross, "Jesus said, 'Father, forgive them, for they know not what they do.' And they cast lots to divide his garments."[164] If that doesn't get you fired up to coach like a soul on fire, I'm not sure what will.

I believe what Jesus said while being nailed to the cross, "Father, forgive them, for they know not what they do," shows God's unmeasurable and indescribable love for us and shows how fortunate we are to be able to live under his grace. Grace is the mercy and love that God has for us and it is something we can never earn. It is something that is undeservingly given to us because God desires us to have it. This is obvious because God in the flesh came down from heaven to show us how much he loved us by taking on the form of a servant, showing us the way, and humbling himself to the point of death on a cross (please reference back to Phil 2:8) to take the punishment and die for our sinfulness.

All we have to do to live under God's grace is to turn to Jesus, believe in him, and recognize that he is our Lord and Savior. We did absolutely nothing to deserve it. And given that we did nothing to deserve it, it is our duty as coaches in Christ to give back to him by serving others with everything we have. Jesus expressed to us that we received without paying, therefore we must give without pay.[165]

Through Jesus' servant leadership (which will be the center of Part III of this book) and through the myriad of miracles that God performed while walking the earth, I believe they can all relate back to Jesus' commandment to us when he stated, "A new commandement I give to you, that you love one another: just as I have loved you, you also are to love one another. By this all people will know that you are my disciples, if you have love for one another."[166]

We have undeservingly received God's grace by the steadfast and never-ending love he has for us, which was shown through Jesus. God in the flesh gave everything he had for us throughout his life. He committed his life to servitude. He was perfect and without sin. And he then withstood the most inhumane and brutal punishment this world has ever seen, *verberatio* (defined as the act of severely beating or striking), before carrying his cross on his back to his crucifixion site. And he was able to continue his final walk to his crucifixion site because of his love and Passion for us.

Jesus, God in the flesh, died for us in the most brutal way this world has ever seen. He died for us so we may live eternally through him. By this sacrifice, we have an obligation to give everything we have for him. And I believe this is done by honoring him through his words on how he wants us to coach and serve others, and that is showing love to one another as he loved us and coaching like a soul on fire every day, because we were fortunate enough to receive something we never deserved: Jesus Christ.

Matt 6:34: "Therefore Do Not Be Anxious about Tomorrow, for Tomorrow Will Be Anxious for Itself. Sufficient for the Day Is Its Own Trouble."

Within our last sub-chapter, we first spoke of one true characteristic that Jesus wants us to exhibit that I believe leads to desired qualities that will allow us to grow as coaches in Christ. That one characteristic is truly asking and wanting him in our hearts (please reference back to Jer 29:13 and John 15:4). By seeking him and recognizing that "He is the key to living life abundantly" (please reference John 10:10), our dependency and faith in him will continue to grow because we have made him our priority. And being that he is our priority in life, we will find it in ourselves to demonstrate our determination, perseverance, and consistent action of serving (coaching) others for him, because he so readily gave everything he had, including his life, to us.

In this sub-chapter, I want to address the one thing that may try to stop us from giving everything we have by coaching for Jesus. The one thing that will always try to bring us down when we want to be lifted up can be summarized in one word. Life. And what is the one common thing that will result if we let life push us around? Anxiety.

Anxiety is something we all fall into, and it is hands down one of the main qualities that tries to stop or hinder our determination, perseverance, and consistent action of coaching the best we can. As our coaching and strength within ourselves goes up, anxiety tries to bring us down. That is the nature of how the world tries to manipulate us into what it wants us to become. For Jesus told us, "If the world hates you, know that it has hated me before it hated you. If you were of the world, the world would love you as its own; but because you are not of the world, but I chose you out of the world, therefore the world hates you."[167] Jesus is telling us that tribulation will come (see John 16:33), hard times will come, and anxiety will attempt to come, but directly after these coaching points, he reminds us, "I have said all these things to you to keep you from falling away."[168] I believe what Jesus tells us in John 16:1 directly relates to maintaining our determination, perseverance, and consistent action. He's telling us that things such as anxiety will try to hinder us, but he tells us to not let these things enter our minds, as it will ultimately manipulate us and hinder us from becoming the best coaches and versions of ourselves. But even though we know to not let anxiety overcome us, how do we do it? Jesus addresses this to us, in Matt 6, when he states, "Therefore do not be anxious about tomorrow, for tomorrow will be anxious for itself. Sufficient for the day is its own trouble."[169]

Typically, anxiety becomes apparent when we let negative thought processes enter our minds that makes us question ourselves and our decisions on the future.

As I wrote this statement regarding anxiety, I looked at it for quite some time and recognized how truthful it can be. When it comes down to it, in almost every situation (but not all) we become anxious when we are thinking of something that may happen in the future and our minds aren't fully engaged on what's actually happening in the present time. Rarely ever do I find myself showing bad anxiety (by "bad anxiety," I mean negative thoughts, not anxiety such as "butterfly's" before an event) if I am fully engaged on what's happening in the present. If we become anxious, we almost always ask ourselves, "What if?" "What if this happens, or what if it doesn't go according to plan? What if I mess up, or what if I do something wrong?"

Constantly thinking or questioning ourselves on something that may not even happen in the future leads us into a state of chronic anxiety, which ultimately inhibits us from putting out our best effort within the present time. There is only one thing we can control for certain, and that is living in the present as best we can so future occurrences will be more likely to come in our favor.

Look at the top coaches and people of influence within the current time, whether that be top athletes, sport coaches, executives, cancer fighters, or the people who continually get up day after day and work as hard as they can to help support their families. What are the things that they all have in common? They all have an objective or a purpose for living, and they all give their best efforts in things they have control over. They know what their objective and purpose is, and they fulfill it by living in the present and displaying their best efforts one day at a time. They don't skip steps within the process.

And this is exactly what Jesus did. He knew his objective, he knew his purpose, and he embraced adversity and lived through his ministry one day at a time. He lived in the present as best he could to accomplish his goal for the future, which was to save us.

Similarly, if we know our objective and purpose and give our best efforts towards the things we have control over and try not to skip steps within the process, we will be better able to decrease our anxiety because we are living within the present, not thinking about negative possible occurrences in the future that most likely won't even become a reality.

I would now like to address something that could become apparent along your coaching journey. It is something that I believe Jesus wanted to show us through his example. As we backtrack a few paragraphs, I said that Jesus embraced adversity and lived through his ministry one day at a time. This addresses the question we may have: "What if I do limit the amount of anxiety in my head by living in the present? I tried to do everything right, and it still didn't come in my favor. What now?"

For this answer, all we have to do is look at the example Jesus showed us through his ministry. At times, Jesus got knocked down, but you know what, he got right back up and kept moving. Anxiety that attempted to come into his head (for example, the anxiety he showed on the night he was unnecessarily arrested in the garden of Gethsemane) was squashed by the level of determination and perseverance he showed towards his purpose. He was living in the present and found it in himself to overcome anxiety by controlling what he was able to. He didn't ask "What if?" He embraced the adversity and turned it into his ultimate triumph.

As mentioned previously, we will experience adversity and things may not turn out as planned. But he has told us, "What I am doing you do not understand now, but afterward you will understand."[170]

I mentioned that top coaches and people of influence within today's society don't skips steps within the process. They embrace every aspect of it. Within our coaching journey and process as coaches in Christ, we have to trust Jesus' plan for us. We must embrace things that still may not go our way. If we embrace minor setbacks and do the best we can to overcome them by living in the present, we will turn these minor setbacks into huge comebacks. If we let anxiety take over our minds, it will hinder us from truly living in the present and it will inhibit us from turning misfortunes into miracles.

As stated before within this book, God will prune us at times so we will produce more fruit and build stronger versions of ourselves. This is how we become stronger individuals. This is how we become better people of influence, and this is how we become great coaches in Christ. The world and the age of anxiety will keep us down if we let it, but by living through Jesus' words and the example he showed us, we can limit our anxiety and take control of our minds, which will allow us to demonstrate our true potential.

Lam 3:22–23: "The Steadfast Love of the Lord Never Ceases; His Mercies Never Come to an End; They Are New Every Morning; Great Is Your Faithfulness."

This is a coaching cue that I hold close because it is a daily reminder and reinforcement of the merciful God we serve. I am the furthest from perfect, and I make mistakes every day. We all make mistakes, some being larger than others. Some of us feel that we have made such big mistakes within our lives that we think to ourselves, "How could he forgive me for what I've done? If he does forgive me, there's no way he would think of me the same." Or we may come to a point in our life when we actually distance ourselves away from God because we are so ashamed of what we have done. This is the exact opposite of what God wants from us. God sent his Son to show us who he is through Jesus' words and by the way he lived.

By living for Jesus, we have to understand that we must accept his forgiveness. If we don't learn to let things go and seek forgiveness, then we will continuously live in a chronic state of guilt, which inhibits us from living in the eternal freedom that God wants for us. Quite frankly, it diminishes what Jesus did for us on the cross. And this is something I have to remind myself of so often. By accepting Jesus, we are accepting his grace. We are accepting that Jesus was the sacrifice for our past, present, and future sins, which allowed us to be acceptable to God by faith through him.

Jesus demonstrates that we should accept his forgiveness and grace in the book of John when he washed his disciples' feet. When he began to wash his disciples' feet, he came to Peter, who seemed confused and said to Jesus, "'You shall never wash my feet.' Jesus answered him, 'If I do not wash you, you have no share with me.'"[171] I believe Jesus is telling us through this example that if we don't learn to accept his grace, which is what his life was about, we aren't fully accepting what Jesus did for us.

Even while being nailed to a cross, he still cried out, "Father, forgive them, for they know not what they do!" (see endnote 164) And while he hung on the cross, "pierced for our transgressions and crushed for our iniquities" (see prophecy written in Isa 53:5), people still mocked him saying, "If you are the King of the Jews, save yourself!" Even the two criminals who were being crucified with him reviled him (see Mark 15:32). But as Jesus' time on earth was ending, one of the criminals still reviled him and mocked him while the other said, "'Do you not fear God, since you are under the same sentence of condemnation? And we indeed justly, for we are receiving the due reward of our deeds; but this man has done nothing wrong.' And he said, 'Jesus, remember me when you come into your kingdom.' And he said to him, 'Truly I say to you, today you will be with me in paradise.'"[172]

At this time, Jesus was brutally beaten from the night of his arrest. He was incredibly sleep deprived having not slept the previous night, and he was extremely dehydrated. He was slayed by being chained to a post and brutally whipped with a flagellum that tore into his insides. He lost an unfathomable amount of blood, and was then crucified. He was then laughed at by "rulers," "soldiers," and the two criminals that were crucified with him. And after the criminals laughed at him, one searched for forgiveness from Jesus and this Man still found it in his heart to forgive him and give him life. While hanging on a cross, he was still thinking of the best interest of other people.

By accepting and receiving God's grace through Jesus, we are able to live under an open heaven, meaning that we are made right with God through faith in Jesus and truly accepting what he did for us. As it is written,

> For all have sinned and fall short of the glory of God, and are justified by his grace as a gift, through the redemption that is in Christ Jesus, whom God put forward as a propitiation by his blood, to be received by faith. This was to show God's righteousness, because in his divine forbearance he had passed over former sins. It was to show his righteousness at the present time, so that he might be just and the justifier of the one who has faith in Jesus.[173]

I mess up and I make mistakes. A lot. But by learning from our mistakes and truly seeking and accepting Jesus' forgiveness, we will always be able to live Passionately with him and for him. For he told us, "All that the

Father gives me will come to me, and whoever comes to me I will never cast out."[174]

By the coaching cue given to us in Lam 3:22–23, and by the example that Jesus showed to us while on the cross, I hope you can see that Jesus will always be with you and he will forgive you. This is the beauty of the God we serve and the Man we live for. By holding on to this coaching cue, I believe it will help us live life to the fullest. And once we know that we will always be made right with God by accepting his grace and believing and living for his Son, we will then be able to live as Passionate coaches for Christ.

Ps 16:8: "I Have Set the LORD Always before Me; Because He Is at My Right Hand, I Shall Not Be Shaken."

This is a coaching cue that can be held close to our heart as reassurance that God will always be with us, no matter what the circumstance. This is a message that I believe can be best explained through example and it is a message which demonstrates that God must be our priority throughout life, and by doing so, we will not be shaken. I first want to talk about who this psalm was written by and then explain a monumental event in his life that we all can learn from. I then want to apply the message to an event in Jesus' life that we can translate to our lives as coaches.

Many of the psalms were written by David, including Ps 16. That's right, the one and only David who defeated Goliath. David was the youngest brother within his family and grew up as a shepherd, meaning he served his assignment by staying in the fields to take care of the sheep every day. But one day, he went to bring food to his brothers as instructed by his father. During this time, Goliath, the Philistine giant, approached the Israelites saying the same thing he had for forty straight days, morning and evening.

> He stood and shouted to the ranks of Israel, "Why have you come out to draw up for battle? Am I not a Philistine, and are you not servants of Saul? Choose a man for yourselves, and let him come down to me. If he is able to fight with me and kill me, then we will be your servants. But if I prevail against him and kill him, then you shall be our servants and serve us." And the Philistine said, "I defy the ranks of Israel this day. Give me a man, that we may fight together." When Saul and all Israel heard these words of the philistine, they were dismayed and greatly afraid.[175]

When David heard Goliath speak, he found it in his heart to take on this giant, for he said, "What shall be done for the man who kills this Philistine and takes away the reproach from Israel? For who is this uncircumsied Philistine, that he should defy the armies of the living God?"[176] David hated that this Philistine intimidated the Israelites because they were God's people. David wanted to take on the challenge of fighting Goliath. When the word got to King Saul, he called for David and told him he couldn't fight him because he is too young. However, David told Saul that he has been a shepherd for his father and when a lion or bear took a lamb from the flock, he struck the predator and delivered the lamb out of its mouth. For David proceeded to say, "'The Lord who delivered me from the paw of the lion and from the paw of the bear will deliver me from the hand of this Philistine.' And Saul said to David, 'Go and the Lord be with you!'"[177]

Even though armor and a sword was given to David, he refused and took only his staff, sling, and five stones from a brook that he put in his shepherd's pouch. As David approached the giant, he (Goliath) thought it was a joke. Goliath was equipped with armor and deadly weapons, while David only had a sling and some stones. He cursed at David and said he would give his flesh to the birds of the air and the beasts of the field. But David said, "You come to me with a sword and with a spear and with a javelin, but I come to you in the name of the LORD of hosts, the God of the armies of Israel, whom you have defied."[178] As the two approached the battle line, David put his hand into his pouch, took out a stone and shot it right at Goliath's forehead, sinking deep into it, leaving him dead. David conquered Goliath the giant with only a sling and stone, and he knew he could do it because he continually placed God at his right hand, and as a result, he wouldn't let anything shake him.

I want us to now reference to a few other verses within Pss 16 and 17, which I believe can directly relate to the symbolic and incredible event that was the battle between David and Goliath. Within Ps 16, David also says, "I say to the LORD, You are my Lord; I have no good apart from you."[179] For David also pleads to God in a prayer in Ps 17, "Keep me as the apple of your eye; hide me in the shadow of your wings."[180] These verses and pleads to God not only pierce our hearts, but I believe they serve as a reinforcement to us that David kept God as his priority. Given that God was David's priority, his dependency on him continued to grow (as you can tell by David's words within the verses above). By setting God at his right hand, he was able to display the necessary determination needed to defeat Goliath because he was so grounded in his faith. These qualities that we discussed in our previous sub-chapters directly relate to David's example. And we can see that if we truly make God our priority and if we continually set him at our right hand, we will not be shaken.

We can now relate the message of Ps 16:8 to Jesus' life and when he was on the cross for us. "At about the ninth hour [about 3:00 pm; he had been on the cross since the third hour, or 9:00 am] Jesus cried out with a loud voice, 'Eli, Eli, lema sabachthani?' that is, 'My God, My God, why have you forsaken me?'"[181] What Jesus is yelling to God is similar to what David expressed in Ps 16 and 17 (see endnotes 179 and 180). Jesus is saying, "I need You! I am no good apart from You! Keep me in the shadow of your wings!"

Sometimes, we may feel forsaken from God or we don't feel like he is with us. As you can see, Jesus even felt this way. But you know what, he didn't quit. He didn't give up. Even when he was nailed to a cross and hung there for six hours, he still kept God, and you and me, as his priority.

"After this, Jesus, knowing that all was now finished, said (to fulfill the Scripture), 'I thirst.'"[182] He said this to fulfill the last prophecy (located in Ps 69:21), in which they gave him sour wine to drink. By this, Jesus knew his mission was completed. After the last prophecy fulfillment, "he said, 'It is finished.'"[183] "Then Jesus, calling out with a loud voice, said, 'Father, into your hands I commit my spirit!'"[184]

The proceeding events fire me up every time. When Jesus gave up his spirit to God, "The earth shook, and the rocks were split."[185] And after his burial, we know his resurrection took place on the third day after his crucifixion.

We can learn so much from these last events in Jesus' life on the cross. Even though Jesus felt forsaken at such a dark time, he still kept God at his right hand in order to complete the mission for God and for us. In the best of times and in the hardest of times, we must always keep God at our right hand and trust in his process, because by doing so, he will lift you up, just like he raised Jesus up through his resurrection. Through God, anything is possible. We can see this through Jesus' example because as he continually kept God at his right hand, immediately after he passed away on the cross, the earth did not shake him, he and God shook the earth.

Phil 4:13: "I Can Do All Things through Him Who Strengthens Me."

This coaching cue within God's word, written through Paul, builds upon our last example and provides proof that you can do all things with Jesus. From the example above, Jesus demonstrated to us on the cross that if you always keep God at your right hand, even in the darkest of times, you will be able to do extraordinary things as coaches and leaders. With Jesus always being at your right hand and by keeping him your priority, instead of you cowering to the earth, the earth will cower to you (as Jesus demonstrated to us when he passed away on the cross).

Paul, who wrote the letter to the Philippians, was living proof to this last statement, in which the example was set by Jesus. Paul continually set Jesus as his rock, his foundation, and he kept him at his right hand after committing his life to him. Paul had one thing in his mind after committing his life to Jesus, and that was spreading the gospel.

Throughout Paul's missionary journeys, he traveled to approximately forty-eight different cities and areas, spanning multiple countries surrounding the Mediterranean, Aegean, Ionian, and Adriatic Seas. He traveled approximately ten thousand miles by foot and boat to spread the good news! Yes, you read that number correctly, that is not a typo. He wanted to spread the word of Jesus no matter what it took, as he was imprisoned, beaten, and stoned in the process. And in fact, thirteen of the twenty-seven letters/books within the New Testament are attributed to Paul. And it's safe to say that Paul's words within the New Testament have had an incredible impact on our faith and the church. With Paul continually keeping Jesus at his right hand, no matter how hard the earth tried to beat him down, he continued to get back up and pursue his goals, for he would not let anything shake his spirit and what he stood for as a man. Paul said that he can do all things through Christ, as we can see that was made true by him accomplishing so much through his missionary journeys, and it was because he continually kept his underlying purpose, Jesus, at his right hand.

With this in mind, I now want to mention the words Paul wrote that preceded Phil 4:13, which gave him the determination and confidence to say, "I can do all things." Immediately preceding Phil 4:13, Paul says, "Not that I am speaking of being in need, for I have learned in whatever situation I am to be content. I know how to be brought low, and I know how to abound. In any and every circumstance, I have learned the secret of facing plenty and hunger, abundance and need."[186]

Paul had become so engrained in his faith, he knew that in every situation he was going to come out on top. In every situation, whether it seems to be an unfruitful season or if he feels on top of the world, Paul never lost sight of his driving purpose and Passion. As we become more engrained in our faith as coaches in Christ, we will experience highs and we will experience lows, just like Paul. We will experience fruitful seasons and we will experience times when it seems that we can't catch a break.

But Paul, who was an incredible leader and coach, demonstrated to us through his arduous missionary journeys that we must go through the valley if we want to stand on the mountain of God. This was demonstrated in Jesus' ministry and through Paul's missionary journeys. But this is how God molds us into who he ultimately wants us to become. At times, he prunes the branches that bear fruit so they may bear more fruit as time proceeds (please reference back to John 15:2). This is how we become stronger versions of ourselves and better leaders and coaches. Speaking of strength, the journey of our faith can be compared to our muscle. Muscle must be broken down in order to become bigger and stronger. It has to experience a stimulus that requires it to adapt so it can become a better version of what it used to be. If we never experienced challenges, if we never experienced times of being low or times of hunger (like Paul said), then we would never be able to recognize the true power of God if we don't keep him with us throughout our journey in its entirety. Through Paul's example, we as coaches and leaders are able to develop the same Passion that he had because "the Spirit of God, who raised Jesus from the dead, lives in you."[187]

Knowing that same power lives in us, we too as leaders and coaches can continue to strive forward in the ups and the downs. Being broken down only made Paul a stronger version of himself as a leader. It allowed the flame in his heart to burn even hotter for his Passion and purpose. It increased his level of determination and perseverance because it was for someone who is so much greater than us. We too can develop the same level of determination and perseverance that Paul did, because the same spirit that lived in him also lives within you and me. And by having the same level of determination and perseverance that Paul did, we too can say without a doubt on our journey, "I can do all things." By having this mentality as a leader and coach, we will not only become stronger versions of ourselves, but this will directly relate to our coaching ability and will allow us to have the greatest impact on others and who it is we are a coach for.

Throughout Part II of this book, we have discussed the coach that we all have within ourselves. We all have incredible potential as leaders and coaches, and that potential is exhibited through and because of the Man that will stand from the beginning to the end. I hope you have learned more about God's word and how he too wants us to become the best leaders and coaches in Christ that we can be, and it all starts by finding the potential we have within ourselves through Jesus.

I hope you have enjoyed Part II and I hope that you have been able to recognize that God is always moving in your life. Let us now transition to Part III and discuss in more detail how we can use the coach within ourselves to make the greatest impact on others and their journey.

Part III—Coaching Others through Jesus' Example

NOW THAT WE HAVE found the true coach within ourselves, let us now discuss in greater detail how we can effectively transition that into coaching others. Within Part III, I want to discuss key coaching qualities that Jesus adopted which allowed him to become the greatest coach this world has ever seen. I am going to write the final part of this book through his example. By this I mean that I am going to talk about various events and acts along his ministry that demonstrated the qualities I am going to talk about.

Part III is going to be surrounded around one word. HEAVEN. This is the acronym I want to use in order to discuss the servant leadership that Jesus showed throughout his ministry. Each chapter will correspond with a letter within the word, HEAVEN, and each letter relates to the quality that Jesus exhibited as a coach. By demonstrating these qualities everyday as we coach others, I believe it will better help us to coach like him. This acronym and the key qualities that Jesus demonstrated throughout his ministry is shown below.

Humility

Effort

Acceptance of Accountability

Virtuous

Enjoyment

Newborn

The six letters within this acronym will comprise the six remaining chapters within this book. Within each chapter, I want to describe events and/or coaching cues that Jesus gave us to use as we interact with and coach others. More specifically, we will discuss specific events or coaching cues that Jesus exhibited which demonstrates the respective quality mentioned within the acronym, HEAVEN.

With that being said, let us now dive into these qualities that will allow us to coach like Jesus with the addition of our faith. Jesus' leadership surrounded around servitude. And in addition to this quality, I believe Jesus coached through a HEAVEN mindset. Let us now go into greater detail of this mindset and start with the first quality within our acronym, which is humility.

12—Humility

THROUGHOUT THE GOSPELS, WE can see that Jesus' ministry surrounded around servitude and humility. Not only do we know this through the myriad of healings and miracles he performed, but he humbled himself to the point of an unfathomable torture and death by going through unnecessary beatings, the process of verberatio, and then crucifixion. And while on the cross, Jesus was still thinking of others (as we have previously mentioned in Part II)! While Mary (his mother) and John (his disciple) were standing by him while he was on the cross, Jesus said to his mother, "'Woman, behold, your son!' Then he said to the disciple, 'Behold, your mother!'"[188] And as previously discussed, Jesus listened to one of the criminals that was being crucified with him, and Jesus still forgave the man and told him that he would be with him in paradise. Jesus showed an unprecedented and unmatched level of humility and servitude that no one will ever match. His life and ministry was a commitment to servitude, and from this statement, this is where we will begin.

I want to begin by referring back to John 13 when Jesus demonstrated an example of humility by washing his disciples' feet. We previously spoke of this event through accepting Jesus' forgiveness, but I would now like to transition to the events that follow. During the Last Supper, when Jesus knew his hour had come to leave the world to go back to God, he took a towel and wrapped it around his waist before proceeding to fill a basin with water. He then began to wash the disciples' feet and wipe them with the towel that he had tied around his waist.

> After washing their feet, he put on his robe again and sat down and asked, "Do you understand what I was doing? You call me 'Teacher' and 'Lord,' and you are right, because that's what I am. And since I, your Lord and Teacher, have washed your feet, you

ought to wash each other's feet. I have given you an example to
follow. Do as I have done to you."[189]

Not only did Jesus show us the example by washing his disciples' feet, but
he directly told them how they should act as future leaders. The example
of servant leadership that Jesus demonstrated throughout his ministry was
and still is the greatest form of leadership 2,018-plus years later, and I am
going to tell you why.

Demonstrating humility shows to those whom you coach that you are
bought into the process. I believe this is very important to establish early
on in your relationship with whom it is you coach. (Please note, throughout
the proceeding chapters, we will refer to those whom you coach as your
"team." Whether that be your athletes, your employees, your colleagues,
etc. You can conceptually apply "team" to who it is you are a coach for.) By
doing so, you, as the leader, are showing that you have both feet in the door
and you are just as much engrained in the plan as you want them to be. It
doesn't matter how great you may think your plan is, you are only effective
if "buy-in" amongst your team is demonstrated.

Now, I am not saying that you need to do everything. That's ultimately
going to overload you and you are going to end up less effective because
you can't do your own job efficiently, which will actually diminish your
effectiveness as a coach and leader. In order to create buy-in, I believe you
must demonstrate that you are willing and able to do whatever it takes to
help your team succeed and move forward.

I want to relate this methodology to a system of gears that are all in-
terconnected. The gears are comprised of various sizes with some being
big, medium, or small. The working gears symbolize your team and you
are the overseer of the working process. If one of those gears stops, it ends
up effecting the entire system, making your plan or system as strong as its
weakest link (we will discuss more of this in the "acceptance of accountability" chapter). If the gear needs an energy spark to get going or if it is
overloaded, you, as the leader and overseer of the gear series, are willing
and able to put in the effort to keep your system a well-oiled machine that
allows the "buy-in" gear series to work. Whether that be helping a "smaller
gear" or a "big gear," everyone is a part of the same series that makes it run
smoothly. For we are told to not think of ourselves more highly than we
ought to think.[190] We understand and know our place within the system as
the leader, but once the plan is established and while we continuously oversee the system, we are just as much a part of it as everyone else. Whether

your team consists of you and one other person, or you and one hundred to five hundred people, you can conceptually apply this gear system method to your team. By applying this mindset and taking this sort of action, you can create buy-in and gain the number one quality needed from your team as a coach, which is respect.

Respect from your team is critically important to develop and it essentially magnifies the buy-in from them. The amount of buy-in that you show to your team by the demonstration of humility and servant leadership will transfer to effort that your team puts out because you are showing that you care about the process. And most importantly, you are honoring an aspect of how God wants us to lead.

As you know, a successful plan cannot be executed alone, and we can't be everywhere at once. Establishing a high level of buy-in amongst your team essentially develops respect in such a way that allows your plan and system of excellence to carry over while you are not there. I believe this can apply to a myriad of situations because we all are different types of coaches, and we all have different situations in which we look to develop our team. For example, if you are a parent, your system of excellence can transfer to your child's study habits while at school, or it can apply to your assistant when you are away and you need him/her to ensure that your daily plan is executed with 100% efficiency, or it can apply to someone you have been mentoring and they applied a system of excellence within every aspect of their lives because of the respect gained towards you as the leader. And this system of excellence was made amongst your team because of the respect you earned by caring and doing whatever it takes to seeing the long-term prosperity of who it is you coach.

I want to build upon this point of caring to see the long-term prosperity of your team through a coaching point that Jesus gave to us, and that was through the miracle of calming a storm. Within this miracle, we need to take note of where Jesus was and what he did following the cry from his disciples. But let's first describe the background and scenario of this miracle (this miracle can be found in Matt 8, Mark 4, and Luke 8).

On that day, when evening had come, Jesus said to them, "Let us go across to the other side." While they were on their journey, a great windstorm arose, and the waves were breaking into the boat. Now, Jesus at the time was in the stern of the boat when his disciples cried out for his help. Jesus, coming to the forefront to support them, was there for his disciples and immediately calmed the storm. The disciples then marveled at what they saw.

I believe there is a key aspect from this miracle that we can learn from as coaches in Christ. It is recorded that Jesus was in the stern (back) of the boat—i.e., he was behind them and was ready to catch them if they fell. Jesus didn't exalt himself to the front. He placed himself in the back and humbly oversaw everyone else. As leaders, we should always be ready to catch someone who looks up to us and considers us their coach or mentor. I want to also note what Jesus told his disciples before they went across to the other side of the lake. He said, "Let us go across to the other side," i.e., "Let us take on this plan and journey, together." Jesus demonstrated that he is a part of the plan in every way, and he was engrained in the process with his disciples. After Jesus calmed the storm, his disciples were amazed and believed in him even more. Through this example, we can see that in order to be a successful leader and coach in Christ, continuously being there for your team will result in respect because of your demonstration of buy-in through humility.

Now please do not think I am taking this miracle out of context. Jesus is demonstrating to us within this miracle that he is the one that is always with us, he is the one that will calm the storm when we cry out to him, and he is the one that will always be with us on our journey. But Jesus calls us to be like him and he has taught us in the way we should go. It is also written, "Whoever says he abides in him ought to walk in the same way in which he walked."[191] With that being said, we can learn to be an effective coach through his example, but we must know that Jesus *is* the example and he is the one that we always look to.

With this in mind, I believe we can now transition to another coaching point from Jesus that directly relates to us as leaders. Throughout the chapter thus far, we have discussed examples that relate to staying humble through what we do and being engrained in every part of the process to create mutual respect and buy-in amongst your team. We have talked about continuing to go and being a part of every gear within the series, but we haven't talked about recharging ourselves in order to stay efficient. If you're coaching like a soul on fire and giving everything you have to your team on a daily basis, there is no doubt that can take a toll on you. There have been times when I have felt like I was starting to sink or times that I felt like I was getting buried. But Jesus reminds us that he is a part of our process just as much as we are. And just like when he calmed the storm, he also reminded us that he is always with us when he walked on water.

You may find this miracle in Matt 14, Mark 6, and John 6. You can also reference back to endnote 47, as we briefly mentioned this miracle there as well. This miracle took place after he performed the miracle of feeding the five thousand.

> Immediately he made the disciples get into the boat and go before him to the other side, while he dismissed the crowds. And after he had dismissed the crowds, he went up on the mountain by himself to pray. When evening came, he was there alone, but the boat by this time was a long way from the land, beaten by the waves, for the wind was against them. And in the fourth watch of the night he came to them, walking on the sea. But when the disciples saw him walking on the sea, they were terrified, and said, "It is a ghost!" and they cried out in fear. But immediately Jesus spoke to them, saying, "Take heart; it is I. Do not be afraid."
>
> And Peter answered him, "Lord, if it is you, command me to come to you on the water." He said, "Come." So Peter got out of the boat and walked on the water and came to Jesus. But when he saw the wind, he was afraid, and beginning to sink he cried out, "Lord, save me." Jesus immediately reached out his hand and took hold of him, saying to him, "O you of little faith, why did you doubt?" And when they got into the boat, the wind ceased.[192]

Within this miracle, we can point out keys aspects that I believe Jesus wants us to learn from. We can see that Jesus let the disciples go across the sea while he dismissed the crowds. Note that this was after his disciples have been with him for some time now and it was after they committed themselves to him. And yes, the disciples dealt with an eventful and challenging storm, but we have discussed in detail that God will put us in tough or challenging situations that will ultimately make stronger versions of our faith and ourselves. And through these situations, he will display his glory to us if we trust him, include him, hear with our ears, understand with our hearts, and turn to him (please reference Matt 13:15). Even though Jesus wasn't physically with them during the heart of the storm, he always had his eye on them (from the top of the mountain). God was putting them in a tough situation that ultimately led them to grow deeper in their faith.

At first, Peter thought Jesus was a ghost! The presence of God can be a petrifying thing, which I believe directly relates to this chapter and how we are all humble servants and coaches in his name. But Jesus then said, "It is

I," and then told him to walk out. Even though Peter began to walk towards Jesus, he still looked at the waves and the winds present, and he began to sink. But Jesus still reached out his hand and grabbed him, saying, "Why would you ever doubt?"

In our coaching journey and in our lives, we always know whom to look towards when things get hard, when we feel overloaded, or when we feel like we are starting to sink from being overwhelmed. But even when the world tells you to look back and it wants to pull you into anxiety (just like when Peter looked back at the waves), Jesus will still grab your hand when you feel overwhelmed or overloaded (you may reference chapter 9 as well). Jesus' disciples abided in him, and he in them. Just like them, we are his sheep, and no one will snatch us out of his hand (please reference John 10:27–28). And after Jesus grabbed Peter, they got back into the boat. "And those in the boat worshiped him, saying, 'Truly you are the Son of God.'"[193]

This hard time, this storm that the disciples were in, led to stronger versions of their faith and of themselves. I wanted to present this miracle and coaching point from Jesus near the middle of the chapter because during your coaching journey, you will experience tough times where you feel overloaded, beaten down, or you may feel psychologically drained from what it is you do. We all at some point in time have experienced one of those three qualities along our path. But we all need to keep in mind that we must go through a valley if we want to stand on top of the mountain. And while we feel like we are in the valley, and when we feel like we are sinking (just like Peter was), Jesus will grab you because of your commitment to him.

With that being said, we need to reference back to the miracle and note that Peter was already walking towards Jesus when he grabbed him. We must always aim to walk closer towards him throughout our process, and by doing so, we will find peace through him.

I believe that to be an efficient leader and coach in Christ, we should try our best to "do nothing from selfish ambition or conceit, but in humility count others more significant than yourselves,"[194] while also doing our job to the best of our ability. There is no doubt that will take a toll on us at times. But we can help withstand that through Jesus' example to us, in which he had an incredible inner circle to help him and he constantly prayed. By having these two key factors to help us (which we outlined in chapter 8 and 9), we can better open our eyes to who it is we serve and our commitment to servant leadership. And we know this is exactly how Jesus coached us and others throughout his ministry.

By having our inner circle and continuously seeking guidance from him through prayer throughout the valleys and mountains, we can now apply our previous discussion to a greater challenge that Jesus calls us to lead by and magnify our topic of servant leadership. For Jesus tells us, "But whoever would be great among you must be your servant, and whoever would be first among you must be your slave, even as the Son of Man came not to be served but to serve, and to give his life as a ransom for many."[195]

Jesus showed us the example that we should demonstrate humility when he washed his disciples' feet. We can also learn from him that we should continuously oversee our team through a humble mindset and be ready to catch our teammates when they fall. Jesus showed this to us when he calmed the storm and was initially in the back of the boat, overseeing the process. We also discussed this through the example of our gear series. We also mentioned that as leaders, we should count others more significant than ourselves while also making sure we do our job to the best of our ability. And while this can be hard, we discussed that we can always seek peace and guidance from him in prayer while also having our inner circle with him as our centerpiece.

Jesus is our centerpiece. I believe that is the one key statement and reminder that allows us to take our coaching ability and servant leadership through humility to the next level. Jesus doesn't just call us to be good. He calls us to be great, and he told us exactly how to do that in the previous Scripture. He said, "Whoever would be first among you must be your slave." And his proceeding statement is a reminder to us that we are coaching for a much bigger purpose. He said, "Even as the Son of Man came not to be served but to serve, and to give his life as a ransom for many." Jesus is the epitome of servant leadership and he humbled himself to the point of death on a cross. From this statement, we realize that what we do as coaches is bigger than ourselves. It's about serving for a greater purpose and seeing our team prosper. I believe by counting others more significant than ourselves by what Jesus stated in Matt 20:27 in combination with doing our own job to the best of our ability, we have found necessary components to becoming an extraordinary coach in Christ.

To conclude this chapter, I want to relate what Jesus stated in Matt 20:27, "Whoever would be first among you must be your slave," to what

Jesus tells us in Luke 14, "For everyone who exalts himself will be humbled, and he who humbles himself will be exalted."[196]

Being humble yet confident and direct when necessary is paramount to developing respect amongst your team. But I believe there is a fine line between being direct (which is clearly necessary to demonstrate that you are the leader and overseer of your team) and exalting yourself. Exalting yourself will give off the impression to your team that they are the ones helping you succeed, which will limit the amount of buy-in your team displays and will diminish the effectiveness of your plan and what you are wanting to accomplish.

Our ultimate goal is to see our team and the others around us prosper. It's important that your team respects and understands that you are the one in charge and you are the leader. No one will respect you if you let everyone walk all over you. But ultimate respect is gained from your team when you show authority when necessary and also demonstrate humility by doing whatever it takes to help your team prosper by being a part of every aspect within your plan and process. By doing so, you will not only help others prosper, but as Jesus said, you will be exalted among others. And most importantly, when our time has come to a close, you will feel confident that God will say to you, "Well done, My child."

13—Effort

NOW THAT WE HAVE essentially set the foundation of the HEAVEN mindset through the demonstration of humility in our coaching approach, we can now move to the next letter within our coaching acronym, which stands for Effort. This chapter will coincide and build off the "Humility" chapter. To describe more specifically, the demonstration of humility within your coaching approach signifies that you are bought into the process and will create respect amongst your team that will allow your plan of prosperity for others to take full effect. In other words, by applying what we described last chapter, you will have an incredible impact on others' lives through your help and through your example. The application of humility as a leader doesn't show that you are the "boss," it shows to them that you are their mentor and you are willing to do whatever it takes to make a positive impact on their lives and help them towards their future accomplishments. But in addition to helping others around you prosper through the common goals that you have as a team, our approach as coaches in Christ is to make a long-lasting impact on our team. An impact that may resonate to other aspects of their lives and who it is they coach (in hopes that you may help indirectly create disciples of all nations through Jesus' HEAVEN coaching approach.)

And while the demonstration of humility will help develop the necessary qualities amongst your team that allow your plan and common goals to manifest, it is continuous effort that adds fuel (effort) to the fire (humility). The greatest leader of all-time, Jesus, continuously demonstrated high-levels of effort in his coaching approach, which ultimately translated to his disciples' effort levels and their common goal amongst themselves as a team (i.e., spreading the gospel). I now want to discuss effort and its importance to our coaching approach through Jesus' coaching cues as well as his example, which helps display to us that we must continually add fuel (effort) to the fire (humility) if we want to continuously thrive as coaches in Christ.

I would like to begin by discussing one of Jesus' coaching cues to us, which is located in Matt 5. While he was preaching, he said, "And if anyone forces you to go one mile, go with him two miles. Give to the one who begs from you, and do not refuse the one who would borrow from you."[197] I love this verse as it is a continuous reminder to us to not just do what is required, but to be all in within our coaching approach. He's telling us to go beyond our call of duty, by putting in the extra effort to help our team excel and prosper towards the common goal.

How does this apply to our lives as coaches? It's being there for a member of your team who needs extra help or if he/she is craving to get better and asks for your assistance. It's displaying your knowledge in a more detailed and personalized manner to a member/s of your team who doesn't understand the material to accomplish the task at hand. It's taking responsibility as a leader to put in the extra work needed for your team to flourish. It's knowing that you're not just going the extra mile for your team, but it's knowing that you are doing it for Someone that is bigger than me and you. It is this statement that allows us to continually add fuel (effort) to the fire (humility). For Paul tells us in Romans, "Never be lacking in zeal, but keep your spiritual fervor, serving the Lord."[198] And it is by applying these first two components of the HEAVEN mindset that allows the fire in our hearts to continually burn, not just for the success of your team as a unit, but for the Man that's the driving force behind what it is we do.

Throughout the preceding paragraphs, I have discussed the fuel to the fire concept and that the demonstration of humility helps us set a foundation for the effort that we put into our team. I want to note what Jesus said before He told us to display effort through our coaching. Directly before he told us to go the extra mile, to give to the one who begs from us, he said, "And if anyone wants to sue you and take your tunic, let him have your cloak as well."[199] In this day in age, we obviously don't wear tunics and this verse doesn't have to directly apply to someone suing you. Jesus wants us to conceptually apply it to our situation and read deeper into its meaning. This is one thing I've learned over time when studying the Bible. It's about reading the word in such a way that allows it to operate at our hearts. As Pastor Steven Furtick said in one of his sermons, "Slow down, read it."

As you read what Jesus says in Matt 5:40, you can see that it directly applies to displaying humility, which comes directly before his coaching cue of telling us to display high levels of effort, which he narrates in Matt 5:41–42. Through Jesus' words, I believe this provides proof to the fuel to the fire concept and how displaying high levels effort builds upon our foundation of humility and effectiveness as a coach.

To be an effective coach in Christ, we mentioned that we should apply what Paul wrote to us in Philippians, when he says that we should count others more significant than ourselves. What this does is first establish to the member/s of your team that you care about them more as a person and not just fulfillment of the task or goal. Demonstration of humility says that you are all on the same playing field, and you are all trying to accomplish a common goal. Again, as the leader, it's about establishing the plan and displaying to your team how exactly you are going to get there. But once the plan/goals are established and you continually oversee the process, you are just as much a part of the plan as everyone else. That's servant leadership. The demonstration of servant leadership contributes and shows to your team that you care about the members first and foremost. This magnifies the buy-in and respect needed for your process to run efficiently. And it is with the contribution of effort that shows to your team that you also care about the process and plan. You must first demonstrate that you care about the member/s of your team as individuals before you care about the plan. Every process and every plan has different aspects that contribute to achieving the common goal (i.e., all members of your team need to do their part to the best of their ability for the plan to be achieved to its greatest capacity). As a result, the effort that you put into them and the process will be magnified and will radiate to others. In summary, first show that you care about the members of your team, then care about the plan and dominating your common goals as a unit.

Throughout Part III, we have essentially discussed qualities that will improve your leadership ability through Jesus' coaching cues and example. Qualities that help set your foundation, establish your brand, and demonstrate that you are all in for your team. We have discussed our fuel to the fire concept which essentially allows our light (flame) to shine, which leads us into Jesus' next coaching cue about effort.

While teaching, Jesus tells us, "You are the light of the world. A city set on a hill cannot be hidden. Nor do people light a lamp and put it under a basket, but on a stand, and it gives light to all in the house. In the same way, let your light shine before others, so that they may see your good works and give glory to your Father who is in heaven."[200]

Throughout the entire book thus far, we have discussed various aspects about finding the true coach we all have within ourselves and how we can apply that to the betterment of our lives and others. Jesus' coaching cue above not only builds upon the effort that he wants us to show through what we do, but it builds upon what we have discussed throughout the entire book. Within Part I, Part II, and Part III thus far I hope you have learned a few things, as I certainly have while I write this book! Through what we have discussed and hopefully applied within your lives, I believe we have essentially intensified the shining light within ourselves. And just like Jesus tells us, there's no point in having a shining light that lives for the truth and keeping it under a basket. By taking what we have learned and applied within ourselves in Part II, Jesus then calls us to display that by living for his word, and I believe all aspects of the HEAVEN mindset. Meaning that we are not only applying what we have discussed in this chapter directly, but we are making a conscious effort to apply what we will discuss in the remainder of this book.

By knowing that we should take our light and apply high levels of effort towards doing the best we can through the HEAVEN mindset and its entirety, let us now go back and zero in on the application of effort towards the betterment of our team.

This next coaching cue from Jesus adds to what we have discussed about going the extra mile for our team and letting our light (which includes the combination of humility and effort, i.e., components to the burning flame) shine towards others. This is a coaching cue that we briefly mentioned in Part I. You may reference this event in John 21:15–19.

While Jesus and Peter were talking, Jesus asked Peter if he loved him more than these (he was speaking of their breakfast). Please also keep in mind that this event took place after Jesus' resurrection. *Awesome!* Peter replied to Jesus, "Yes, Lord; you know that I love you." Jesus then said, "Feed my lambs." He then asked Peter the same question a second time, resulting in the same answer from Peter. Jesus then said, "Tend my sheep." Yet again, Jesus asked Peter if he loved him, and Peter said, "Lord, you know everything; you know that I love you." Jesus said to him, "Feed my sheep." And after their conversation, Jesus then said, "Follow me."

It must be noted that before their conversation ended, Jesus told Peter, "When you were young, you dressed yourself and walked wherever you wanted, but when you are old, you will stretch out your hands, and another will dress you and carry you where you do not want to go." Following this, the word tells us, "Jesus said this to show by what kind of death Peter was to glorify God." (As stated earlier in this book, it is reported that Peter was crucified upside down because he felt that he wasn't worthy to die in the same manner as Jesus.)

There are three key points that we can learn from Jesus within this coaching cue to Peter. First and foremost, Jesus essentially tells Peter, "Coach my people with 100 percent effort. Feed my lambs and tend my sheep the way I have shown you. You know the true coach in Christ that lives within you (Part II), now go out and give everything you have for our purpose and goal." We must also note that Jesus told Peter to "feed his lambs" or "tend his sheep" three times! I don't know about you, but when someone reminds me to do something three times, it's probably pretty important. Jesus is telling Peter that in order to be the great leader I know you have inside you, you must continually display high levels of effort towards the goal. As coaches in Christ, we must also continually display high levels of effort while we lead our team. It is imperative that we never let the fire in our heart go out, just like Paul says.

Now I'm not saying it's easy, but it's definitely easier to display high levels of effort for your team when everything is going right. But I believe what truly defines a great leader is when the chips are down and your back is against the wall, and you still put in the necessary effort you know you need to in order to get the job done. When your team is in need, they are going to look to you, the leader, to minimize the issues at hand or make the necessary adjustments to succeed as a unit.

Jesus addresses this directly after he tells Peter to display high levels of effort towards the goal. He reminds Peter that it is going to get hard and you will experience situations that you don't want to be in. But as previously mentioned, great leadership is about continuing to lead your team, taking charge, and displaying the necessary authority to get out of the tough times. Yes, Jesus was talking about the death that Peter would go through to glorify God, but this is a reminder to us that as coaches in Christ, we lead in the great times, hard times, and everywhere in between. Remember, every word that Jesus spoke has a deeper meaning to it and how we can apply it to our lives. Just like Pastor Steven Furtick said, "Slow down, read it."

After this reminder to Peter, and us, Jesus says, "Follow me." He's saying within the tough times, within the hard times, continue to look at him. He wants us to communicate with him directly through prayer. But remember, when Jesus says, "Follow me," it also means to continue to follow his word for answers as well. This is true because at the beginning of the Gospel of John, it reads, "In the beginning was the Word, and the Word was with God, and the Word was God. . . . And the Word became flesh and dwelt among us, and we have seen his glory, glory as of the only Son from the Father, full of grace and truth."[201] Jesus was God in the flesh, and this verse signifies that Jesus was the word. So, when Jesus says, "Follow me," he wants us to also be in the word as well as communicating with him directly.

When the chips seem to be down for us, we must continue to lead with 100 percent effort and be the authoritative figure that your team will look to. But as Jesus reminds us, it will get tough at times. He wants us to continually push forward and he also reminds us that we must follow him throughout the process and we always have him and his word to look to, in all circumstances.

Now that we have discussed coaching points from Jesus about displaying high levels of effort in our leadership, we can now transition to the high levels of effort that he displayed through his example.

This specific topic cannot be broken down into three to five situations. As you know, the examples and coaching cues that I am mentioning and discussing are nowhere close to the myriad of examples that Jesus taught and displayed throughout his ministry. They do directly relate to the topic discussed and they directly relate to the quality that Jesus wants us to exhibit in our lives and coaching approach. But they are just a small portion of the brilliance and wisdom that Jesus displayed. I wanted to mention this directly because there is no way I, or anyone, could list out all the different situations in which he displayed high levels of effort. If we mentioned only three situations in which he displayed high levels of effort without recognizing that he did display this coaching quality in many more ways, I feel that I would be doing somewhat of a disservice for everything he has done for you and me.

The examples of Jesus' high level of effort are endless. He healed the sick and paralytics, he cleansed the lepers, he healed blind men, he healed people who were unable to speak, and he fed thousands upon thousands of people. He did everything and anything he could to express his teachings to crowds, while also teaching his disciples in the way they should go, so we may also learn the way we should live. And he displayed the highest level of effort this world has ever seen in order to show how much God loves us. He was brutally beaten and scathed before crucifixion, and this Man still forgave and was still thinking of others while being nailed to a cross. Jesus knew his plan and he knew his goal. He was going to do anything it took to lead and show his people how much he cared for them. He was hanging on the cross while others were watching him.

Our leader, Jesus, did everything he needed to with 100 percent effort in order to save us. There is no question that he is the epitome of displaying 100 percent effort while leading. And he displayed this incredible amount of effort because of the love he has for us. We obviously can't do what Jesus did. We aren't God. But he is showing and telling us that in all we do, give everything we have to it. For he tells us in John 13:34, "Love one another: just as I have loved you, you also are to love one another." By the example he displayed to us through his high level of effort, we should also display that, for the love of our team, our goals, and most importantly, for Jesus.

There is one more thing that I want to mention specifically about Jesus' high level of effort. In so many of his healings and miracles, he went out of his way to do them. By this, I mean that he alternated his current path for someone that needed him. (You may follow along in Mark 10:46–52.)

While Jesus was leaving Jericho with his disciples and a great crowd, a man named Bartimaeus, who was a blind beggar, was sitting on the roadside. When Bartimaeus heard it was Jesus, he cried out, "Son of David, have mercy on me!" Many people then rebuked him, telling him to be quiet. But he cried out all the more, "Jesus, Son of David! Help me!" Jesus then stopped and said to call him. Jesus said, "What do you want me to do for you?" And Bartimaeus then said, "Rabbi (teacher), let me recover my sight." And Jesus said to him, "Go your way; your faith has made you well." Immediately he recovered his sight and followed him on the way.

The key thing we can learn from this situation is that in the midst of what seems like a busy time, you need to make time for the things that go beyond the goals that your team has set. As previously discussed, the members of your team need to know that you care about them as people before you care about the goals you have. No one can get to the top or recognize their true potential by themselves. If you don't care more about the members of your team compared to the goals you have set as a unit, that will show and you will get below average results at best because it limits the amount of buy-in and respect that the members of your team have towards you.

We need to consider how Bartimaeus called Jesus. It says that he "cried out" to him. And he did it more than once. This signifies that Bartimaeus desperately needed him and his help. When a member of your team needs you and your help in certain situations, such as asking for advice or they need someone to be there in a tough moment in their life, you need to make time for them. This goes beyond the typical goals that you and your team have set. It is by applying Jesus' coaching cues and examples thus far that will allow you to develop that respect and trust from your team. This signifies that you aren't just their leader or coach. It signifies that you are viewed as a mentor and someone that he/she can look to in other aspects of life. By making time for things that truly matter, you gain even more respect, which adds to the buy-in that your team will exhibit and as a result, the effectiveness that your team will display as a cohesive unit.

It is by these coaching cues and examples from Jesus that we can learn from in order to become an effective coach in Christ. By applying what Jesus taught us through his high levels of effort, we can add to our HEAVEN mindset coaching approach, which allows us to become more like him.

14—Acceptance of Accountability

As we transition onward through the HEAVEN mindset, we now come to a key quality that Jesus continually displayed throughout his ministry. It is a quality that he tells us to adopt, and it is a key component to how God wants us to live. In addition to the other qualities discussed thus far, Jesus also displays this quality not only through his direct coaching points, but through his example as well.

Just like the qualities we discussed in the two previous chapters (humility and effort), Jesus also displays this next quality throughout his entire ministry. And that quality is the "acceptance of others accountability." And we know that Jesus always accepted the accountability of others through forgiveness. Just as I mentioned last chapter, Jesus' ministry and life surrounded effort. I also said that I would feel like I would be doing a disservice if I didn't state that there is no way I could list the myriad of events, miracles, and healings that Jesus did that showed his incredible amount of effort. I stated that the examples and coaching points we discussed do relate to the quality Jesus displayed, but they are nowhere near all of them. Just like last chapter, I want to discuss multiple coaching cues and examples, but they do not compare to the immense amount of forgiveness and love that Jesus showed. Jesus' life centered around forgiveness. As we know, that's why he died on the cross for us. But God loves us, and he sacrificed his only Son, that whoever believes in him should not perish but have eternal life (see John 3:16).

Knowing that forgiveness was a key component to Jesus' life, we need to dive into some situations and coaching cues from him in which we can learn from. It is by these coaching cues and events that we should not just apply to our leadership ability and approach, but to our entire life (just like the other qualities discussed). With that being said, let us move to the Gospels and discuss examples that we can conceptually apply to the HEAVEN mindset and within our life.

You may follow along specifically in Mark 5:21–34. This event begins when Jesus crossed to the other side of the sea by boat, where a large crowd gathered about him. It was at this time when Jairus, a ruler of the synagogue, came to Jesus asking to save his daughter, who was at the point of death. While Jesus was walking with Jairus, a woman who had suffered from a discharge of blood for twelve years heard about Jesus and followed behind him. She then touched his garments in hopes that she would be made well. Immediately, she had been made well and her disease was gone. Jesus, perceiving in himself that power had gone out from him, turned around and said, "Who touched my garments?" As Jesus was looking around to see who had done it, the woman, knowing what had happened to her, came in fear and trembling and fell down before him and told Jesus the whole truth. He then said to her, "Daughter, your faith has made you well; go in peace, and be healed of your disease."

I would like to immediately jump to Luke 7 and discuss a similar example so we may see the commonalities between the two. (You may follow along directly starting on Luke 7:36.)

One day, one of the pharisees asked Jesus to eat with him, in which he accepted and proceeded to go to his house. And behold, a woman of the city, who was a sinner, learned that Jesus was at this man's house and brought an alabaster flask of ointment, and standing behind him at his feet, weeping, she began to wet his feet with her tears and wiped them with the hair of her head and kissed his feet and anointed them with the ointment. The pharisee who invited Jesus to his house was greatly taken aback as he said to himself, "Does he know who this woman is? For she is a sinner." Shortly after, Jesus said, "Do you see this woman? I entered your house; you gave me no water for my feet, but she has wet my feet with her tears and wiped them with her hair. You gave me no kiss, but from the time I came in she has not ceased to kiss my feet. You did not anoint my head with oil, but she has anointed my feet with ointment. Therefore I tell you, her sins, which are many, are forgiven—for she loved much. But he who is forgiven little, loves little. Jesus then said to her, "Your sins are forgiven, your faith has saved you; go in peace."

There are two things that we can take away from these events. First and foremost, they both came to Jesus in desperation. They both felt that they did something wrong in which it was eating at their conscience. And secondly, even though they showed accountability of their actions slightly different (one kneeling in fear and trembling while the other was weeping), they both sought out forgiveness for their perceived ill-advised actions.

I believe the second commonality between these two events is a very important aspect that we need to take into account. The two women, even though it was shown slightly differently, showed incredible honesty and sincerity in their accountability towards their actions. What the two women demonstrated was not fake. And as a result, Jesus put their sins to rest and moved forward. Just like Jesus, we also ought to forgive the members of our team that are accountable for their actions.

We all make mistakes. I do daily. But it is recognizing those mistakes and learning from them so we can grow and become better leaders. By accepting accountability of your own actions, you are essentially presenting the quality of humility because you are recognizing that you aren't perfect. By showing accountability in a sincere and genuine way, the humility presented will result in high levels of effort to get better and become a better leader. If you didn't catch that, you can see that the acceptance of accountability related back to our two previous variables within the HEAVEN mindset in a positive way, which will lead to greater respect given not only to that individual seeking forgiveness from his/her actions, but to you as the leader if you also hold yourself accountable.

This statement is true by the words Jesus spoke in our last example, "Therefore I tell you, her sins, which are many, are forgiven—for she loved much. But he who is forgiven little, loves little."[202] If we as leaders truly accept the accountability of others, not only will we earn greater respect, but we can read from Jesus' statement that if we don't learn to accept the accountability of others, the love that our team has for us will be less, which results in diminished levels of effort and buy-in towards the goals you have as a cohesive unit.

Let's give an example. Say you felt as if you were doing your job extremely well by putting in your best effort towards your assigned tasks because you had a great respect for your authorities and leaders. You especially admired your direct superior's high levels of effort and you appreciated their desire to lead by example. However, even though you have been going above and beyond your call of duty, one day you happened to make a mistake. It was a mistake that seemed to be fairly detrimental. But it was an honest mistake that you know you could learn from to get better because you aspire to emulate the great example that your superior is trying to set.

As soon as you made the mistake, you felt horrible. You didn't want to hold anything back and you wanted to let your superior know the mistake you made. You are thinking that it is going to be tough to swallow your pride and let him/her know what happened, but you are also thinking he/she will understand and everything will be alright.

As you speak to your manager in a genuine and sincere way and you are accepting accountability for what you did, your leader ends up getting furious. He/she completely bypasses the fact that you didn't mean it, it was a mistake, and you will do your best to not let it happen again. Your superior interrupts you while you were accepting accountability for what you did, and he/she says, "I don't have time for this. I have so much work to do. Thank you for throwing all this extra work on my plate. Please leave now." As your superior became extremely upset from this honest mistake, he/she sent you away feeling ashamed and misunderstood because you know you have been giving your best efforts towards the team or organization. This not only leaves you feeling mad, it results in a lost respect and love for your superior because of the belittlement he/she showed towards you.

From this scenario, we can see the team leader is attempting to put his/her best foot forward for the organization by giving his/her best efforts and getting the necessary work done. But it seems that the leader is so caught up in trying to chase the product, that he/she forgot about the process and the people associated with it. From this situation, you will undoubtedly look at your superior differently. And even though you must bite your tongue and continue to push forward because it's your job, the cohesiveness and efficiency of the team's goals will drop.

As we have stated before, no one gets to the top alone, and as you can see from this scenario, your diminished respect for your leader will result in diminished future efforts and buy-in towards the organization. In the short term, this may not be the case because you as a team member must put your best foot forward and continue to do your job to the best of your ability. But in terms of long-term prosperity and success for the team, it won't work.

We mentioned that the leader in this example was so concerned about the product and high levels of effort, that he/she forgot about the process and the individuals that are associated with it. The leader was quick to speak and quick to anger, which resulted in negativity that could be detrimental to future efforts. But as leaders and coaches in Christ, the word tells us to do the exact opposite of what this leader displayed. In the letter of James, it reads, "Know this, my beloved brothers: let every person be quick to hear, slow to speak, slow to anger."[203] If we don't abide by this coaching cue, it could result in something that we may deeply regret in the future, such as the example given.

We as leaders can display all the other qualities within the HEAVEN mindset, but if we don't forgive and accept others accountability, our team members love and respect for us will drop, just like Jesus told us in Luke 7:47. This will inevitably result in an inefficient process, which limits the aspired results of the product. Everyone makes mistakes. If we don't learn to listen and be understanding, the aspired vision of your team could drastically change in a negative way.

In addition to this point, if we don't accept others accountability, we must look ourselves in the mirror and recognize that we are not perfect. In the previous example, if you were the leader that ended up sending away the team member mad and misunderstood, wouldn't you want to be forgiven if you were a team member who tried to present accountability towards their actions? Even though the mistake was discouraging, we must put ourselves in their shoes and treat others with the respect and understanding that we would also want. For it is written, "And as you wish that others would do to you, do so to them."[204]

This also directly relates to a coaching cue that Jesus gave to Peter when Peter asked, "'Lord, how often will my brother sin against me, and I forgive him? As many as seven times?' Jesus said to him, 'I do not say to you seven times, but seventy-seven times.'"[205] Jesus' life and ministry centered around love, mercy, and forgiveness. Even in the toughest of moments, he still found it in his heart to forgive.

For we mentioned back in chapter 11 that while Jesus was hanging on the cross, one of the criminals was accountable for his actions, saying his punishment was just and he was receiving his due reward for his actions. He was deeply sorry and just asked Jesus to remember him. In the hardest moment in Jesus' life while being crucified, he still forgave the man. Talk about the epitome of walking the walk and talking the talk! I'm not sure who came up with that phrase, but it sure does match up perfectly with Jesus!

Accepting the accountability and repentance of others was an attribute (not the only attribute, but a component) as to why people loved and respected him so much. Great leaders are willing to accept the accountability of others who are sincere while also being able to listen, stay patient, and be slow to anger, specifically in times when it may seem difficult to do so. This is not only written to us in Jas 1:19 (endnote 203), but these are all qualities that Jesus wants us to emulate so we may prosper in his name.

Now, we have discussed various examples, coaching cues, and scenarios that you may conceptually apply to your life and related situations. Given that Jesus always wants us to find it in our hearts to forgive, as hard as that may seem at times, we must learn to do so as coaches, leaders, mentors, and as human beings. For Jesus tells us, "For if you forgive others their trespasses, your heavenly Father will also forgive you, but if you do not forgive others their trespasses, neither will your Father forgive your trespasses."[206]

Through what we have described thus far, we know we can gain respect from our team members from accepting their sincere and genuine accountability, in which they are truly seeking repentance and willing to get better and learn from their mistakes. This will not only result in developing a greater relationship with that team member (you can conceptually apply this to your team and scenario), but it can result in greater efforts in all aspects of your process from that individual, leading to a better and more efficient product.

Now that we have discussed the acceptance of accountability, its importance, and qualities that are directly associated with it, we must also discuss times in which it is best to move on from certain team members when necessary by discussing various coaching cues that will help us to make those decisions. It is certainly never easy to move on from a team member. But if that team member acts like a cancer to your organization or team and he/she is habitually negatively affecting the process, or he/she performs a drastic act that may be inexcusable for your team, you know as the leader it is time to move on from them because they are hindering the desired product and goals of your team as a cohesive unit. (It is my hope that you can apply these coaching cues to your life situation if necessary. For example, you would never move on from your child or your family. But as a leader or coach in your place of work or other aspects of your life, I hope you may conceptually apply them to your plan or path, as we all have a different story to present.)

I want to discuss this matter because while reading, you probably asked yourself, "Is this guy saying that no matter what someone does, even if they hold themselves accountable, I have to forgive them and act as if everything is alright? No matter what, I need to forgive them and keep them on my team?

From Jesus' actions, should we always forgive? The answer to that question is *yes*, based off Jesus' standards and by the example he set for us. But while forgiving someone, does that mean that they should continually be a part of your team, even if it doesn't seem right in your heart? The answer to that question is *no*. As a coach and leader, we should understand that we must do what is best for our team as a unit. If you have given an individual multiple chances to learn from their serious mistakes and they continue to disrespect your process, or if an individual commits an act that would inevitably take away from the integrity and standard of excellence that you are continually trying to set for your team, then you know it is best to end that relationship.

Throughout the book thus far, I hope you have learned that our journey as coaches is about the process and setting a standard of excellence not just for your team, but for you as an individual. And it's about creating a culture that works with and for each other so your team continues to run and work at a high efficiency. Our previous elements to the HEAVEN mindset discuss servant leadership in addition to continually exhibiting high levels of effort, which inevitably creates greater buy-in and respect from your teammates. And we know that the combination of these attributes will equate to achieving the desired product. But in order to obtain those goals that your team sets out to accomplish, everyone must be bought into the process. If everyone buys in on a daily basis, the results will speak for themselves.

With all of that being said, if someone doesn't respect your process by the example you are trying to set through the attributes we have discussed thus far, you must move on from that individual/s. Your process is something you should take pride in because it surrounds principles and standards that you want to hold yourself accountable to as well. Your process doesn't just apply to your place of work, it applies to your life. And if someone doesn't respect or appreciate that, you know as the leader you made the right decision in moving on. As Jesus said, "Behold, I am sending you out as sheep in the midst of wolves, so be wise as serpents and innocent as doves."[207]

People deserve second chances, but you must guard your integrity and what you stand for. If you don't, then your team will second-guess you as their coach and leader, which could take away the respect you've earned from others. Don't let people take away from that. As it is written for us, "Do not be deceived: 'Bad company ruins good morals.'"[208]

Did Jesus always forgive? Absolutely. But did Jesus' team always remain intact? No. Look at Judas. Now, I am absolutely not comparing any member of your team to Judas, the one whom betrayed Jesus. That's obviously unethical. But what I am doing is making a point. I am making the point that things can change. If a gear within your system continually stops, it affects every other gear, which hinders your process. After so long or after an inexcusable event (that is at your own discretion), you need to change that gear so the series can run efficiently.

If a situation such as this arises, we as leaders still need to be able to forgive that person or group of individuals. That is what Jesus called us to do. And even though it is in the best interest of your team to move on from that individual/s, the fact that you are truly willing to forgive and put those things behind you should result in a mutual respect for the future. If not, you know that you took the high road and made the correct decision for you and your team.

We have discussed various scenarios within Jesus' ministry, coaching cues from his word, as well as other examples that you may conceptually apply to your life within this chapter. We have discussed situations in which we should accept the accountability of others and learn to listen to their predicament or situation at hand so they can still be an effective member of your team. We also mentioned the possible consequences if we don't. And we have also discussed situations in which we should still accept the accountability and repentance of others, but also know when to let them go and move on. We should also understand that accepting others accountability can directly relate to and affect the other elements and attributes within the HEAVEN mindset coaching approach. With that being said, let us now move on to the next quality that we should exhibit as coaches in Christ and leaders, which is continually displaying a virtuous behavior and mentality.

15—Virtuous

VIRTUOUS. ONLY ONE WORD, yet it can relate to so many others. Words such as pure, righteous, upstanding, principled, moral, exemplary, upright, and ethical. There are so many powerful and beautiful words that can describe Jesus' ministry. But through the synonyms given, I firmly believe that virtuous could make a case for being in the top five to describe it. Every synonym of virtuous directly relates to everything that Jesus did. He lived without sin, he was always honest, he always practiced and preached morality, and he served as the Man we all should look up to and emulate. His teachings, examples, and actions continually demonstrated virtue. And given that Jesus tells us to learn from him (see Matt 11:29), we should always do the best we can as coaches in Christ to demonstrate virtuous behavior and high moral standards. It is the essence of Jesus' teachings and ministry, and this is why it is included within our HEAVEN mindset coaching approach.

Within this chapter, I want to describe various examples and coaching cues that Jesus displayed and taught to us that demonstrate virtuous behavior. Throughout the teachings, coaching cues, and actions from Jesus that we have described thus far throughout the entire book, we can clearly see that Jesus was virtuous. It is within this chapter that I want to build upon those things and add to what Jesus did and said so we may become more effective coaches. I also want to discuss how Jesus' virtuous behavior led to his team emulating the culture he wanted to establish, which ultimately resulted in the success of their plan as a collective unit, which we know was to further spread the gospel. After all this information is presented, I want to then relate these teachings to possible repercussions if we don't apply them to our lives as coaches and leaders. With that being said, please know that I am not implying that you *must* adopt these things that I am telling you. I am not attempting to point the finger and say, "You have to do this." That would be quite silly because I have no authority to do such a thing.

And that would be hypocritical on my part because there are many times that I mess up. We all do. But what I am trying to do is describe teachings that Jesus gave to us that will be an asset and benefit to our lives. Jesus calls us to be like him and to follow him. Jesus came so we may have life and have it abundantly (see John 10:10), and it would certainly be in our best interest if we adopted a virtuous behavior like his. That's what he wants us to do and calls us to do. It is my hope that by discussing more of Jesus' teachings and coaching cues that demonstrate virtue, you can conceptually apply them to your life as a coach in Christ.

I want to first discuss a parable that Jesus shared to us, which is written in the Gospel of Luke. It is a lesson that I'm sure we are all familiar with, and that is the parable of the good Samaritan (you can follow along in Luke 10:25–37). This parable begins by a lawyer asking Jesus how he shall inherit eternal life. Jesus then asked the man, "What is the law and how do you read it?" The man answered by saying, "You shall love the Lord your God with all your heart and with all your soul and with all your strength and mind, and your neighbor as yourself." Jesus then told him, "You have answered correctly; do this, and you will live."

But the lawyer wanted to justify himself and asked Jesus, "And who is my neighbor?" Jesus then began to explain the parable by telling him that there was a man who was going from Jerusalem to Jericho, and he fell among robbers, beating him and leaving him half dead. And while the man lay there helpless, a priest was going down the road, and passed on the other side. And likewise, another man went down the same road, passing on the other side, avoiding the man. But a Samaritan, as he journeyed, came to where he was, because he had compassion towards him. The Samaritan then proceeded to bound up his wounds, set him on his own animal and brought him to an inn and took care of him. The next day he gave the innkeeper two denarii (a denarius was a day's wage for a laborer) and told him, "Take care of him, and whatever you spend, I will repay you when I come back."

Jesus then said to the lawyer, "Which of these three, do you think, proved to be a neighbor to the man who fell among the robbers?" He said, "The one who showed him mercy." And Jesus said to him, "You go, and do likewise."

To continually be an effective coach and leader, based off this parable from Jesus, we must always count every member of our team as our neighbor. By conceptually applying this parable to your team and your life's situations, you are essentially counting every member of your team as family. This is important to take into account because we previously stated that in order to create complete buy-in and respect, you must establish amongst your teammates that you care about them as individuals before you care about the process or collective goals. If you only care about the process and end goals while displaying mediocrity towards a "neighbor-based" mindset like Jesus described, you will get mediocre results. In other words, you as the leader and coach can create the most brilliant methodology and game plan to achieve your team's collective goals, but the process and proceeding results are only as good as the buy-in and respect that the members of your team show towards you and your plan.

Because I firmly believe complete happiness within yourself, buy-in, respect, and success as a leader comes through adopting the HEAVEN mindset coaching approach in its entirety (which is what Part III of this book is about), at this time, we are specifically talking about the "V" acronym. So, by counting every member of your team as your neighbor, you can continually improve not only your team, but yourself as well in primarily two ways.

1) By conceptually applying the parable of the good Samaritan to your life's situations and leadership approach, you can develop a greater amount of respect amongst your team members towards you, which will enable your team members to work harder for you and your process because they realize that you care about them before anything else. I can absolutely attest to this statement because I have worked for coaches in the past that have treated me as family. And as I look back at those days, they were demonstrating a "neighbor-based" mindset towards me. They were willing to help me and they cared about Michael Roman as the individual first and foremost. As a result, I developed such a respect for those coaches that I was willing to give everything I had for them on a daily basis. I was extremely bought into their program and I was willing and wanting to go the extra mile for them. And throughout the process, I can firmly say during that time we made a pretty good team.

2) By adopting a "neighbor-based" mindset (within the "v"irtuous acronym), our relationship with God can continue to grow. By diving into Scripture, we can find this to be true. By displaying a "neighbor-based" mindset, we are living the way Christ wanted us to and are displaying purity in heart towards our team members. As Jesus said in the Sermon on the Mount, "Blessed are the pure in heart, for they shall see God."[209] And by

committing our team's works for the greater purpose, we are expressing the love that we have for him. By loving one another through the example given in the parable of the good Samaritan, we are living by what Jesus said in John 14:21, which states, "Whoever has my commandments and keeps them, he it is who loves me. And he who loves me will be loved by My Father, and I will love him and manifest myself to him." I believe these two verses (Matt 5:8; John 14:21) can be linked by what Jesus told us, "For to the one who has, more will be given, and he will have an abundance." By committing our works to him and by displaying purity in heart by living through his commandments and standards, he will continue to manifest himself into our lives because of our faith. Hence, to the one who has, more will be given. (Again, I am the furthest from perfect, and I mess up a lot. But I try to live by this and I am a living testimony to that statement as I know so many of you are as well.)

The next coaching cue from Jesus directly relates to the parable of the good Samaritan and applying this mentality within our lives and leadership approach. I can say with complete affirmation that by applying what we have discussed in Part III thus far, greater respect, buy-in, and effort will be exhibited towards you and your process to achieve your team's collective goals. Why am I so confident in this statement? Because Jesus (the most successful Man to ever live) and his words are still alive, living, and standing 2,018 years later and counting. For he told us, "Heaven and earth will pass away, but my words will not pass away."[210] He preached the truth, lived the truth, and has shown us how to implement the truth within our lives. And by implementing the truth within our lives, specifically as it relates to our "neighbor-based" mentality, we not only have the ability to have a positive effect on our team and its process for Jesus, but we have the ability to have a positive effect on him directly as well. What do I mean by this?

As it relates to the beaten man in the parable of the good Samaritan, Jesus essentially relates himself to this man. If we turn to where Jesus discusses the final judgement, he states, "And the King will answer them, 'Truly I say to you, as you did it to one of the least of these my brothers, you did it to me.'"[211] This statement proceeded what he told his sheep (or people that followed his words to the best of their ability). He told these people, "For I was hungry and you gave me food, I was thirsty and you gave me drink, I was a stranger and you welcomed me, I was naked and you clothed me, I was sick and you visited me, I was in prison and you came to me."[212] Jesus is comparing the beaten man in the parable of the good Samaritan to himself.

Throughout all the examples given in the previous verse, essentially, he is comparing the member of our team who needs our help, to himself. Jesus is essentially saying to us, "By showing this love towards others, you are showing that you love Me." This allows us to realize that we are not only doing the best we can to efficiently guide our team through the process, but this "neighbor-based" mindset ensures that we are also continually doing it for our greater purpose.

As the leader and coach, it is paramount that you establish a culture. A culture in which each individual is willing and able to demonstrate humility, effort, accountability, and virtue. If you push these qualities to your teammates by your desire for excellence and passion through your example, your team members will follow your lead. They will mimic your behavior. And boy, if you have every member of your team on the same page by displaying a "neighbor-based" mindset in which everyone helps and pushes each other to achieve the common goal, you have a key ingredient to the recipe of success. But in order for everyone to buy in to this approach, we as coaches need to partake in committed action every day, by creating this system of excellence through our example. For your team as a collective unit to present qualities such as virtue and respect towards each other to achieve the common goals, it must be shown through your example consistently. Your team will adapt to the culture you desire to establish, but only *if* you first establish it within yourself on a daily basis.

For the word tells us,

> For this reason, make every effort to supplement your faith with virtue, and virtue with knowledge, and knowledge with self-control, and self-control with steadfastness, and steadfastness with Godliness, and Godliness with brotherly affection, and brotherly affection with love. For if these qualities are yours and increasing, they keep you from being ineffective or unfruitful in the knowledge of our Lord Jesus Christ. For whoever lacks these qualities is so nearsighted that he is blind, having forgotten that he was cleansed from his former sins. Therefore, brothers, be all the more diligent to confirm your calling and election, for if you practice these qualities you will never fall.[213]

To break this statement down, we must first state that Jesus taught Peter in the way he wanted him to go. Jesus, as the coach and leader, demonstrated virtue, knowledge, self-control, steadfastness, godliness, brotherly affection, and love on a daily basis. He never shied away from the principles and standards he wanted to establish. That ultimately led Peter and the rest of Jesus' team to adapt to the culture he wanted. Hence, Jesus' team member (Peter) wrote the above Scripture (2 Pet 1:5–10) and encouraged others to also display these qualities, which ultimately led them to accomplishing their team goal of spreading the gospel. This statement from Peter provides proof for my previous statement, "Your team will adapt to the culture you desire to establish, *if* you first establish it within yourself on a daily basis." Jesus lived the virtuous qualities just described every day, and it resulted in much prosperity of his team because they too adopted and preached these qualities continuously and were absolutely bought into the process.

Secondly, when we look at verse 8, it states that we must not only possess these qualities, but we must increase in them. (As just described, we need to practice them every day in order to firmly establish our desired culture. This will be further discussed in our "newborn" chapter.) It then states that by practicing these qualities, they will keep us from being ineffective and unfruitful in the knowledge of our Lord Jesus Christ. And as much as we all mess up, we know that Jesus' two most important commandments are to love God with all your heart, soul, mind, and strength and to love your neighbor as yourself. By truly living these two commandments, we are demonstrating that we have the knowledge for how Jesus wants us to lead, which inevitably results in adopting a virtuous behavior. So in essence, by practicing and increasing in these qualities described by Peter, we are increasing in the knowledge of Jesus because we are living the way he called us to. And by increasing in the knowledge of our Lord Jesus Christ, we are also increasing in the qualities that provide the foundation for an extremely effective leadership and coaching approach.

Through the example that Jesus set, Peter was then encouraged to say that those who lack these qualities are so nearsighted that they are blind, having forgotten that they were cleansed of their former sins. This is a statement that directly relates to the parable of the good Samaritan. As we previously described within his teachings, Jesus said, "Truly, I say to you, as you did it to one of the least of these my brothers, you did it to me." He said, "When I was hungry you gave me food, when I was thirsty you gave me drink." And as we previously mentioned, Jesus said these things while describing the final judgement. What is similar between the parable of the good Samaritan, Jesus comparing himself to the teammate in need of help within that parable, and what Peter wrote? Well, Jesus described the parable of the good Samaritan prior to the comparison of himself to the beaten man. And within the Scripture written above in 2 Pet 1, Peter says that we must maintain these qualities *after* he describes them. In other words, Jesus is telling us that we must *maintain* our virtuous qualities not when it just seems convenient to us, but we must permanently embed these qualities within ourselves and who we are as coaches and leaders. Jesus is saying that in unfruitful seasons, prosperous times, and everywhere in between, he calls us to maintain consistent action towards the process. And to paraphrase, Peter then essentially tells us, "Don't forget what you are going for. Don't lose sight of your bigger purpose and the reason behind what you do." It's not just adopting these qualities, it's about maintaining these qualities and not losing sight of the process and the reason behind your coaching and leadership. That's what virtuous and exemplary leaders do, they maintain consistent action towards what they believe in and the process that is accompanied with that. And with the Passion of Christ that lives inside you, nothing in this world will stop you. For Peter concludes the above Scripture by saying, "If you practice these qualities you will never fall."

Now, given that you are reading this book, there shouldn't be any reasons that would give you "cause to pause" or second guess yourself from adopting these qualities that Jesus and his teammate, Peter, described. Jesus lived the truth, preached the truth, and told us how to implement the truth within our lives. He told us, "Everyone then who hears these words of mine and does them will be like a wise man who built his house on the rock."[214] In Matt 4:4, Jesus is referring to every word that comes from the mouth of God (i.e., all Jesus' actions and words throughout his ministry), which includes implementing the mentality of the parable of the good Samaritan and what Jesus taught to Peter and his teammates.

If we don't adopt these qualities within our coaching approach (and within our lives as a whole), we will slip. This is true because if you show inconsistencies in the culture that you are trying to develop amongst your team, you will get inconsistent and mediocre results because you are setting an inconsistent standard within yourself. And if you are setting an inconsistent standard within yourself, you can't expect any of your teammates to rise to a high level. This essentially compares to building your foundation or leadership approach on sand. So, when floods come or adversity hits (as described in Matt 7:24–27), your team will not be absolutely committed to your process. And being that your process and plan is only as good as the buy-in and commitment amongst your teammates, the belief in you as the coach and leader will crumble if you show inconsistencies. This leads to a deterioration of the team cohesiveness needed for success. So, if your team isn't functioning as a single unit, the foundation will crumble and the house that you are trying to build will fall.

It is by consistently displaying a virtuous behavior within our coaching approach that will allow us to become desirable models of leadership. It is by the consistent action of displaying an exemplary behavior that others will follow our lead. By conceptually applying what I have discussed in this chapter, in addition to the other aspects described thus far within the HEAVEN mindset coaching approach, you will succeed within your team's process and goals because it is the way Jesus, the most successful leader of all-time, called us to lead. With that being said, in order for us to continue to prosper for the long-term, we must love what we do. We have to enjoy the process associated with the desired goals. This will allow us to stay true to the other variables within the HEAVEN mindset and will allow us to live life to the fullest and have satisfaction within ourselves. Let us now discuss enjoyment, the critical component that essentially holds the other variables within the HEAVEN mindset together.

16—Enjoyment

WITHIN PART III THUS far, we have discussed key qualities that Jesus demonstrated which allowed Him to be such an effective leader and coach. And as Coaches in Christ, we are able to better emulate these qualities if we adopt the HEAVEN mindset coaching approach in its entirety. Thus far, we have discussed humility, effort, acceptance of accountability, as well as maintaining high moral standards via adopting a virtuous behavior. In addition, we have continually stressed that the process is more important than the product because if we neglect the working parts (our team members) and the variables that create continuous buy-in and respect towards you and the collective goals amongst the team, we will inevitably get mediocre results. As coaches and leaders, we should always have high standards for ourselves and our team. We should always set out to achieve the highest goals as a unit and set out to accomplish those goals every day. But it is understanding the importance of the process and running in such a way to get that prize every day that matters.

And through Part III, we are essentially focusing on the process by discussing each variable within the HEAVEN mindset in detail (or to the best of my ability) individually. Notice that the first "E" within the HEAVEN acronym wasn't "enjoyment." It was "effort." I wanted to place "enjoyment" near the end of our coaching mindset because as we travel through our process (i.e., understanding Jesus' coaching approach), we must not forget to enjoy what we do. While you and your team chase the goals you have set out to achieve, you have to be internally satisfied in your quest to reach those goals. Now, nothing easy is worthwhile and nothing worthwhile is easy. That statement is not even up for debate. If you want to succeed, you have to put in hard work and make sacrifices. And in the world we live in, the most successful people within their scope of practice are quite frankly, obsessed with what they do. Jesus was the epitome of these variables for success. He was obsessed in his goal to spread the good news. He put in an unfathomable amount of hard work in order to do it, and he made the ultimate sacrifice for us to accomplish it, himself. To be successful, we have to show obsession, hard work, and make sacrifices. (Obviously not yourself. We are not God. I wanted to mention his sacrifice for us in order to make a point.) But if we are continually on the grind by being obsessed with our team's success, we make sacrifices for the betterment of our teammates, and we continuously put in hard work day after day without enjoying the process, we will burn out. Those three qualities are paramount for success, but we have to enjoy it along the way.

Let's put it this way because I'm a sports guy. If your starting pitcher has been on the mound all game and has been throwing absolute gas all night with his pitch count over a hundred with a three-run lead (we will assume he has given up a few hits), it would probably be in the best interest for his health to take him out so he will be ready for his next start and increase his chances of staying healthy for the remainder of the season. If his pitch count every game exceeds what he is capable of, he will either throw out his arm or become less effective over time, i.e., he will burn out. It is up to the head coach or manager of the ball club to manage his number of innings pitched and total pitch count so burn out or injury does not occur.

We can directly relate this example to our process as coaches. The athlete's hard work on the mound is synonymous with our demonstration of the variables discussed within the HEAVEN mindset thus far to the best of our ability. And managing the athletes rest is equivalent to our enjoyment of the process. Could you apply this to taking a step away for a short period of time to clear your head? If you need to, yes. This could certainly be the case because if you effectively apply the other variables within the HEAVEN mindset (particularly exhibiting high levels of effort and virtue) towards your team, you probably developed the respect from your teammates to carry out your process with efficiency while you are away. Or, you may have found what you do as a leader so enjoyable, you desire to keep your foot on the gas to continue to help your team. However you conceptually apply it to your life, the key component (especially to the last example) is enjoyment. If you don't enjoy what you do, you will burn out or you will become exposed. This can directly relate to what Jesus taught us: "for out of the abundance of the heart his mouth speaks."[215]

What we have discussed in Part III requires a transformation. Continual application of a servant leadership mentality with the inclusion of high effort, accountability of ourselves and the acceptance of others, as well as maintaining high moral standards is a tall task. There's no denying that. And if we don't find enjoyment within the process associated with our goals, it will continue to eat at us until we break (i.e., out of the abundance within our hearts our mouths speak). Or, your efficiency in the coaching variables within the HEAVEN mindset will decrease, limiting the effectiveness of your team and leadership ability. To put in a real-life example, this means that you may say something you will ultimately regret or you will stress yourself out so much that you may break down. But to learn and cope with these possible situations, complete application of what we discussed in Part II in addition to finding enjoyment in the process will ensure that we are operating at full capacity. For as it is written, "A joyful heart is good medicine, but a crushed spirit dries up the bones."[216]

This proverb is essentially telling us that enjoyment is the glue that holds the rest of our HEAVEN mindset variables together. A joyful heart keeps our engine running. It keeps our minds sharp and firing at all cylinders. As a result, it further helps us lead others in the way we want them to go because of our desire to fully display the leadership qualities discussed thus far to the best of our ability. Whereas if we are crushed in spirit, burnt out, or feel that we are going nowhere, it will eat us alive until it buries us to the point of giving up.

We have briefly discussed possible repercussions if we do become burnt out and the associated negative effects it will have on our leadership ability. And we have briefly mentioned that finding joy in what we do is paramount in order to maintain the HEAVEN mindset for the long-term. Let us now dive a little deeper into the variables and the underlying cause of why we may be lacking enjoyment in what we do at times.

A lot of times, lack of enjoyment comes from the feeling of unfulfillment. And if you have this feeling of unfulfillment within your heart, you may question yourself when things get hard or when things don't seem to add up, and this ultimately leads you to ask yourself if you are doing the right thing. If you are in the right position. And as just mentioned, if this occurs, it will eat you alive over time until you break or give up. And before that breaking point actually occurs, you feel extreme pressure or you will be crushed in spirit throughout the process. It is this feeling of unfulfillment with our associated process that I believe leads to this snowball effect of the other variables. The feeling of unfulfillment leads us into questioning ourselves and our current position, which could come from multiple things—for example, and as just mentioned, when things get hard or when things don't seem to add up in our favor. This leads us to thinking that we are ultimately doing the wrong thing or in the wrong position as leaders, which inevitably misleads us into thinking that we are going nowhere. As a result, we lose enjoyment in what we do, we become ineffective, negative pressure overtakes us, we feel crushed in spirit, burnt out, and we then give up.

We must continually remember that once we commit our life to God, he will establish our steps (please reference Prov 16:9). Having committed our works to him, everything that encompasses our journey as coaches, from the mountains to the valleys, is for a reason and it is not only to mold us into the person we are truly capable of being, but to serve as a role model and exemplary leader to others to help maximize their true potential. And the only way to serve as the coach you are capable of being and the exemplary leader that God calls you to be is by being internally fulfilled through him.

I gave the example earlier of taking a step back for a short period of time if needed to help maintain peace within yourself. This is something we may need at times to help maintain balance. We have to remember, even Jesus needed time to himself. He also had to clear his head so he could maintain his focus of displaying his HEAVEN mindset. As we discussed in depth in Part II, he did this by continually going to desolate places to pray. Jesus had to step away after the best of times (i.e., after the feeding of the five thousand) and in the hardest of times (i.e., in the garden of Gethsemane) to help maintain his focus and purpose. And it is recognizing that God provided the internal fulfillment needed for Jesus to continually succeed and persevere.

Within our lives and within our coaching journey, there will inevitably be ups and downs. There will be times when things are firing at all cylinders for you and it is a very fruitful time within your life. But there will also be times when you won't enjoy a particular moment or season. Quite frankly, that is reality. We have all experienced them. However, it is embracing the challenges and enjoying our process as a whole that matters. A great leader is the one who is able to maintain a high level of efficiency throughout the process in its entirety. This can directly relate to what Paul said to us in the letter to the Philippians. "For I have learned in whatever situation I am to be content. I know how to be brought low, and I know how to abound. In any and every circumstance, I have learned the secret of facing plenty and hunger, abundance and need."[217] From this statement and through recognition of Paul's journey, we can see he was able to endure the highs and lows because he was internally fulfilled with Jesus Christ as his driving force.

In this day in age, there are a lot of things that can provide short term fulfillment or enjoyment. And if we don't have a reason behind what we do as coaches, it will most likely lead to empty values that we continue to chase but can never reach. There is nothing wrong with chasing things that accompany what you define as success. I do. I don't know about you, but I want to be the best I can possibly be and make the most out of every opportunity that I am given. We should all try to continually progress in life (and we all define that differently). I know you most likely already are, but if not, I hope this book is encouraging you to do so.

But the key thing to recognize within this success is for whom we do it. The Man that provides the internal fulfillment that gives our hearts peace and satisfaction throughout our process in its entirety. If we neglect who brings us that joy, we are ultimately missing the boat and the whole point in this book. For if we continually draw near to God, he will draw near to us.[218] He will provide us the internal fulfillment that is required so we can keep pushing and keep striving for the success of you and your team. And by finding fulfillment and trusting in the Man that will stand from the beginning to the end, "The LORD will guide you always; he will satisfy your needs in a sun-scorched land and will strengthen your frame. You will be like a well-watered garden, like a spring whose waters never fail."[219] It is by this that we may know that everything is for a reason. It is by this that we shouldn't question our journey when things get hard or things don't go in our favor. In those seasons that are hard, it is knowing that God will bring us out of that sun-scorched land. It is being internally fulfilled by Jesus that allows us to be content (just like Paul said) in every circumstance. It is through Jesus, that we may have the light of life (see John 8:12).

As previously mentioned, there will undoubtedly be seasons within our journey that don't seem enjoyable to us. There will be stressful times that we will encounter in which the world will want us to question ourselves as leaders, ultimately leading to a snowball effect of negative variables that try to lead us into giving up. However, "You are a chosen race, a royal priesthood, a holy nation, a people for his own possession, that you may proclaim the excellencies of him who called you out of darkness into his marvelous light. Once you were not a people, but now you are God's people; once you had not received mercy, but now you have received mercy."[220]

Throughout the chapter thus far, I believe this Scripture written by Peter is the epitome of our internal fulfillment of Jesus which allows us to continually find enjoyment through what we do as coaches. Throughout the entire book thus far, it is obvious that Jesus burning in our hearts is where our enjoyment and fulfillment comes from. There is nothing else in this world that will bring us the true internal fulfillment that Christ does. He is ultimately our Gateway to Glory, the Truth, and the Way to eternal life. And before we get to him, he wants to be a part of our process!

"Delight yourself in the LORD, and he will give you the desires of your heart."[221] I believe by truly delighting in him, this first means that he is our priority and we abide by his standards. If he comes first in all aspects of our lives, then he will establish our steps. This gives us the reassurance that everything is for a reason and it is to help mold you into the coach and leader that God wants you to be. So even in the midst of adversity and stressful times, we can still find it in our hearts to push through and enjoy the process because no matter what the circumstance, God has your journey mapped out.

And it is by this that we may be internally fulfilled with our process, limiting or eliminating the "snowball effect" qualities associated with feeling unfulfilled in our hearts. By taking a step back and recognizing the bigger picture, we can see that throughout the hardships or storms, it's all a part of the process and God is always on your side because just like Paul said, "You are God's people and you are in his possession." And as Scripture also reads, "Everyone who believes in him will not be put to shame."[222] That's what keeps our engines running. That's what keeps a smile in our hearts. With every day and moment, as coaches and leaders, we have the opportunity to help others recognize their true potential and we have the ability to help lead our team to success. It's about leaving a legacy and being remembered for having a positive impact on who it is you coach and knowing within yourself that you gave everything you had, because it is for someone who is much greater than us.

If you feel that you have done that, you will have true internal fulfillment within your heart because it's for the Man that is calling you into his eternal glory. I believe that is how we as humans find everlasting enjoyment throughout the process when things get hard or when things seem incredibly confusing. It's always great to enjoy the fruitful seasons and we should cherish those prosperous times, but it is through this that we are able to find enjoyment and be internally fulfilled throughout every aspect of our journey. By continuing to abide in him and he in us, all things will work together for good for those who love God and are called according to his purpose (please reference Rom 8:28). That's how we find true joy and that's how we are able to continue to push and maintain the HEAVEN mindset coaching approach for the long-term.

For Jesus said, "You are the salt of the earth, but if salt has lost its taste, how shall its saltiness be restored? It is no longer good for anything except to be thrown out and trampled under people's feet."[223] Jesus is saying that we are his chosen people and we are his sheep by having our ever-growing faith in him. It is all the variables within the HEAVEN mindset that gives us our saltiness, and by being internally fulfilled through Jesus, we can maintain them. It is continually living and coaching for him that will prevent us from losing our taste. Because if we lose it or fall away, if we fail to see the bigger picture for what we do, we will lose our effectiveness of being the best coaches we can be because we won't display the qualities that Jesus calls us to use within his leadership approach to the best of our ability. And he said quite frankly, "You will be thrown out and trampled under people's feet." i.e., mediocrity amongst yourself will arise, ineffectiveness could surface amongst your team, and you won't be able to display your potential as a leader.

It is through the internal fulfillment that Jesus gives us which allows us to continually let our light shine before others. It is through him that we can maintain our saltiness. And through this fulfillment and what has been discussed within this chapter, we are able to find everlasting joy through-out the process by taking a step back and recognizing the bigger picture through what we do. We must realize that on the other end of the valley is a mountain. And we must go through multiple valleys and mountains within our lives before we can stand on the ultimate mountain of God. Through this fulfillment within ourselves, we can find enjoyment within our process. By this, you can continue to be the effective leader that God calls you to be. He wants you to enjoy and be renewed within your spirit every day. This leads us into the final component within the HEAVEN mindset coaching approach and will be the final piece of this book. In order to continually serve Jesus to the best of our ability, I believe we should also be newborn every day and make the most out of every day we are given.

17—Newborn

I believe it is through the HEAVEN mindset coaching approach that we are able to truly coach like Christ. By demonstrating humility through a servant leadership approach, displaying high levels of effort, accepting the accountability of others as well as ourselves, adopting an unwavering virtuous behavior, as well as being internally fulfilled in our hearts by Jesus, we can better become like him in everything we do. And it is by this internal fulfillment that we are able to find true enjoyment within our lives. As we have discussed each of these qualities in detail, we must not forget that within everything Jesus did, he was incredibly steadfast. He lived and breathed everything he taught. Jesus walked the walk and talked the talk every single day. And it is by this reminder that we will conclude Jesus' HEAVEN mindset coaching approach. In order for us to continually coach for Christ, we have to bring our 100 percent every day for him and for our team. It is through Jesus' example that God calls all of us to be incredible coaches and leaders in his name. And we can see that Jesus wants all of us to succeed and make a positive impact on others and our team. But to truly live up to what Jesus calls us to do, we have to show consistency in our leadership approach. Because if we aren't consistently striving for greatness amongst ourselves and our team, we will ultimately be content with complacency. And it is by this complacency and stagnation that will ultimately lead to mediocrity, which is the exact opposite of what Jesus calls us to be. As previously mentioned, Jesus tells us, "For truly, I say to you, if you have faith like a grain of mustard seed, you will say to this mountain, 'Move from here to there, and it will move, and nothing will be impossible for you'" (please reference back to Matt 17:20). (If you haven't already, I highly encourage you to look up the growth of a mustard seed. The smallness of a mustard seed compared to what it is able to become is incredible!)

But in order to reach that true potential that we all have stored within us, we have to give our 100 percent every day as coaches. If we continually set our minds on things that are above and do not lose heart or become complacent, we can truly become the leader that Jesus calls us to be. Jesus continually set his mind on things above, he never lost heart, and he never became complacent. And through his outstanding leadership, it led to the members of his team believing in themselves. This is clearly apparent throughout the New Testament, as we can see that Jesus' team was able to do the impossible by becoming better versions of themselves through Jesus' coaching ability and leadership approach. And just like him, we can do the same by renewing our spirit (newborn) every day and trying to be better than yesterday. With the mentality of treating every day as an opportunity to get better, you will truly be able to move mountains because if you have the mindset to continually coach for Christ and maintain him as your driving force, that mustard seed that is your faith and coaching ability will continue to grow.

As just mentioned, Jesus continually set his mind on things above. He was constantly deep in prayer, as we discussed in detail in Part II. And within this chapter, it is particularly important to reiterate that Jesus started his day with God. Before he efficiently displayed the other variables within the HEAVEN mindset coaching approach, he prayed in solitude in the morning to keep his coaching ability operating at full capacity. We can see this is clear by turning back to Mark 1 (which we have previously mentioned in Part II), where it reads,

> And rising very early in the morning, while it was still dark, he departed and went out to a desolate place, and there he prayed. And Simon and those who were with him searched for him, and they found him and said to him, "Everyone is looking for you." And he said to them, "Let us go on to the next towns, that I may preach there also, for that is why I came out." And he went throughout all Galilee, preaching in their synagogues and casting out demons.[224]

As this Scripture was given in Part II through our discussion of when Jesus prayed and how we can incorporate it into our lives, we can now add to this discussion having detailed the variables within the HEAVEN mindset. When Jesus prayed in the morning and started his day with God, we can see from the Scripture above that it enabled him to continue to operate at full capacity because after he prayed and was renewed, he was further empowered to say, "Let us continue on so I may coach others in the way they should go. Let us continue on so we can conquer our goals as a team, and let us continue on so we can win the day.

Directly after Jesus started his day with God, we can see that he was able to present the variables within the HEAVEN mindset to a great degree. For example, after he told his disciples, "Let us go on to the next towns," a leper approached Jesus, imploring him to make him clean. As Jesus was greatly moved with pity, he stretched out his hand, touched the man, and he was immediately healed. Immediately after, Jesus instructed him to say nothing to anyone.[225] Through this example, we can see that Jesus wasn't trying to be recognized, he wasn't trying to make a scene. Even though God in the flesh healed a man of a disease by simply touching him, Jesus humbled himself by not boasting of his works. Jesus is saying to us that he wants us to do our work to the best of our ability, but to stay humble within the process.

> Thus says the LORD, Let not the wise man boast in his wisdom, let not the mighty man boast in his might, let not the rich man boast in his riches [humility], but let him who boasts boast in this, that he understands and knows me, that I am the LORD who practices steadfast love [through our HEAVEN mindset, this is continuously presenting high levels of effort towards our team by treating others as more significant than ourselves; see Phil 2:3], justice [acceptance of others' accountability], and righteousness [adopting an unwavering virtuous behavior]. For in these things I delight, declares the LORD.[226]

We can see that through this Scripture, Jesus is wanting us to emulate what has been discussed throughout Part III thus far.

And as we can see, after Jesus started his day with God, he immediately demonstrated the first characteristic within the HEAVEN mindset. But he didn't stop there. As we proceed into Mark 2, it is written that

> And when he returned to Capernaum after some days, it was reported that he was at home. And many were gathered together, so that there was no more room, not even at the door. And he was preaching the word to them. And they came, bringing to him a paralytic carried by four men. And when they could not get near him because of the crowd, they removed the roof above him, and when they had made an opening, they let down the bed on which the paralytic lay. And when Jesus saw their faith, he said to the paralytic, "Son, your sins are forgiven."[227]

From this passage, we can also see that Jesus accepted the man's account-ability because of the group's sincerity and need for help. And it was after this that he healed the paralytic and helped the man in need, which is an example of Jesus presenting virtuous behavior by doing the right thing to help the man. (But we must recognize that this obviously doesn't just ap-ply to helping our team members when they need it, but to conceptually demonstrate an unwavering virtuous behavior within our lives and coach-ing approach.) And within all this Scripture presented, Jesus was internally fulfilled by God, giving him the ultimate satisfaction that only he can give.

As it is clear that Jesus demonstrated the HEAVEN mindset through-out the Gospels in their entirety, I wanted to discuss the Scripture imme-diately proceeding Mark 1:35 (which states to us that Jesus started his day with God through prayer) to show you that by being renewed in our Spirit every day, we can keep our focus where it should be, which allows us to maintain and demonstrate the qualities within the HEAVEN mindset to the best of our ability (as Jesus showed us even in the example that is pre-sented in Mark 1 and 2).

There is one more thing that I want to point out within this Scripture that we can learn from. In Mark 2:1, it states, "He returned to Capernaum after some days." It is after this statement that he continued to demonstrate the other aspects of the HEAVEN mindset. i.e., Jesus was steadfast in his coaching approach by renewing himself through prayer with God every morning. He didn't present significant ups and downs. "After some days," he continued to stay steadfast towards his leadership approach. This is what helped him stay grounded and focused in the process, as Jesus calls us to emulate this example. And it is apparent through the Scriptures presented in Mark 1 and 2 that Jesus first renewed his mind (newborn) by starting his day with God. And it is after this that he was able to efficiently display all the other variables within the HEAVEN mindset. Now that we have estab-lished this through Jesus' example, we can now relate it to our lives.

In this day in age, there are so many things that are trying to pull our minds in a million different places and there is no doubt that we live in the age of anxiety. And if we let this chronic anxiety take over our lives, it will inhibit us from operating at full capacity. Given that we are now on a topic that this world tries to pull us into, I must point something out that is very simple, yet profound. I need to state that this is attributed to Pastor Steven Furtick, as he preached this in his sermon titled, "When Anxiety Attacks." Look at what's in the middle of the word anxiety. Can you see it?

Yes, that's right, it's the letter "I." Pastor Furtick tells us that at the center of our anxiety, is our pride.

I want to add to his statement as we can relate this to our HEAVEN mindset. If we allow this world to pull our minds in so many directions, we will fall into this trap of chronic anxiety. And it is through this anxiety that we resort to asking or telling ourselves, "How am I going to get everything done today? How can I continue to coach or lead effectively with all these other things going on? There is no way I can do this." And as you can see, each of these three statements are centered around "I."

Every leader needs his/her own coach. Jesus even needed a coach to help him (God). We have to recognize that even though we now understand the variables that make a great leader, we cannot express these qualities to the best of our ability alone day in and day out. We must keep Christ as the keystone in our process by continually being renewed in the spirit of our minds[228] every day. If we don't, it will be easier to fall into complacency, mediocrity, and stagnation. By being "newborn" every day and starting our day with God, we will be able to "let the peace of Christ rule in [our] hearts, since as members of one body [we] were called to peace."[229] And it is the peace and internal fulfillment of Christ that allows us to recognize that what we do is for a greater purpose, not just for ourselves. It is about living through him so we can have a lasting impact on the members of our team and accomplish the collective goals as a unit.

As we continue on through this chapter, I want to compare it with continuing on in our journey as coaches. We have discussed it within this book already, but like most of us, I always need to be reminded to stay patient in times that seem frustrating, bleak, or unfruitful. At times within this book, we have discussed the highs and lows that we will inevitably encounter as coaches and how to best deal with them through God's word and Jesus' example. I want to add to these previous discussions now that we are detailing the last component of the HEAVEN mindset. I, as well as you, have dealt with hard times and tough situations. These situations could be outside of your position as a coach or they could be directly affiliated with your team members. Whatever that situation may be, whether it tries to bring frustration inside of us or anxiety that inhibits us from leading effectively, there will be multiple events that will try to steer our minds in the wrong direction.

But I want to reiterate what Jesus did day in and day out. He always started his day with God through prayer and he was firmly steadfast in his process while on earth. He never wavered or ran away from the times that brought him grief. He embraced the challenges that were presented to him by remaining true to the HEAVEN mindset. And he was able to do so by renewing his spirit every morning with God in prayer, which enabled him to stay patient through those challenging times. For example, he stayed patient with his disciples when they showed little faith and he stayed patient on the night he was arrested in the garden of Gethsemane, when he literally felt the weight of the world on his shoulders. He was able to stay patient because he was so firm in his faith and he knew everything was going to be okay very soon (i.e., by dealing with the pain he went through, he was crowned champion after his resurrection).

By renewing our spirit every morning through prayer, we can continue to improve our relationship with God, deepening our faith. And as we become deeper in our faith, we will realize that we cannot do anything without it. This is what builds patience, trust, and hope during tough times and it keeps us grounded throughout our process in its entirety.

> [The LORD] does not faint or grow weary; his understanding is unsearchable. He gives power to the faint, and to him who has no might he increases strength. Even youths shall faint and be weary, and young men shall fall exhausted; but they who wait for the Lord shall renew their strength; they shall mount up with wings like eagles; they shall run and not be weary; they shall walk and not faint.[230]

Jesus does not grow weary and he will never faint away from us. We can read that he gives power to those *who wait on him*. We have to always remain steadfast to Jesus, just like he did with God. If we don't hold fast to renewing our spirit, which gives us the power to stay patient through tough times, we will be more susceptible to fall into anger and will be quick to make a wrong decision by losing patience. And it is by losing our patience do we become anxious and lose our effectiveness as coaches.

By continually renewing our spirit and remaining steadfast to him, it will turn out better than expected. When Jesus had to display an unfathomable amount of patience the night he was unnecessarily arrested, it turned out perfect (his resurrection). This example directly relates to the Scripture just given in the book of Isaiah. No matter the situation, Jesus put his trust in God and waited on him because he was so engrained in his faith. And sure enough, he was able to soar like an eagle.

Just like Jesus, we as coaches have the ability to soar. We have the opportunity to start our day with God by becoming newborn in our spirit every day, which allows us to realize that in order to coach for Christ, we can't do it alone. God helped Jesus through difficult times by helping him develop the patience needed to not let anxiety overcome him. It is by the night Jesus was arrested in the garden of Gethsemane that we can see that hard times will come in our lives, which will inevitably try to push us into chronic anxiety. We will all deal with our own Gethsemane, our own situation that tries to lead us into chronic anxiety that will try to make us ineffective leaders. And if we don't renew our spirit by spending time with God (through prayer or reading the word, for example), we will be more susceptible to lose focus on our driving force and become stagnant in our faith, which I believe opens the door to anxiety and pride taking over us. And the less time we spend with God, we will inevitably dig ourselves into a deeper hole that is surrounded by these unfavorable qualities until we break down. But if we continually run to Jesus like children[231] and recognize that we need him as the centerpiece of our lives, chronic anxiety and pride won't take over us, as we can clearly determine that these two unfavorable qualities are the exact opposite of the HEAVEN mindset. And again, what is at the center of the words anxiety and pride? That's right, the letter "I." It is by being newborn every day will we deepen our faith and eliminate the "I" from being the center piece of our lives. This will help keep our eyes on our only true source of enjoyment and life. I believe once we recognize that he is essentially our life by identifying the true coach within ourselves, we will truly be able to coach for Christ through his HEAVEN mindset in its entirety for the rest of our lives. By doing so, I truly believe we will run in such a way to get the prize every day. And when it's all said and done, we will be able to see Jesus when that time comes and he will say, "Well done, my child."

Endnotes

Part I: The Journey

1. See Matt 28:19.

Chapter 1

2. Ps 34:18.
3. See Matt 13:15.

Chapter 2

4. See "Passion," https://www.merriam-webster.com/dictionary/passion.
5. Eusebius, *Eccl. Hist.* 4.15. From Eusebius, *Eusebius: The Church History*, edited by P. L. Maier (Grand Rapids, MI: Kregel, 1999).
6. See Matt 27:24.
7. Matt 27:32.
8. See John 3:16.
9. See John 14:6
10. Phil 2:7–8.
11. Gen 1:3.
12. Gen 1:4.
13. Gen 1:16.
14. John 8:12.
15. John 8:14.
16. See Exod 3:2.
17. Exod 3:13–14.
18. See John 8:51.
19. John 8:53.
20. John 8:56–58.

21. Rev 22:12–13.
22. See Rev 22:16.
23. See Jer 31:33.
24. See John 10:10.
25. See Luke 23:46.
26. Ps 69:21 NIV.
27. Rev 22:7.
28. See Isa 53:5.
29. See Luke 18:1.
30. Matt 17:20.

Chapter 3

31. Jer 29:12–13.
32. John 21:15.
33. John 21:18.
34. Luke 18:6–8.
35. 2 Pet 3:8.
36. Matt 7:24–27.
37. See John 14:21.
38. See Matt 22:37–40; 12:30–31; Luke 10:27; Deut 6:5.
39. Heb 11:1.
40. See Heb 12:1–2.
41. See Deut 31:6.
42. John 14:12–14.
43. Please refer to endnote 38; see also John 13:34.
44. Luke 10:28.
45. See Rom 8:28.

Chapter 4

46. See Luke 5:16.
47. See Matt 14:22–33.
48. See 1 Thess 5:16–18; Heb 11:6.
49. See Matt 15:30.
50. See Heb 11:6.
51. See 1 Sam 26:23.

Chapter 5

52. See Jer 29:11.
53. Eccl 3:3, 7. See generally vv. 1–7.
54. Gal 6:9.

Chapter 6

55. See Col 3:2, 17.
56. See John 13:34; Matt 28:19.
57. Matt 16:21–23.
58. Jer 17:7–8.
59. See Rom 12:12.
60. Prov 3:5–6.
61. 1 Cor 9:24 NIV.

Part II: The Coach Within

62. Rom 12:5–8.

Chapter 7

63. Matt 3:15–17; see also Mark 1:9–11; Luke 3:21–22; John 1:29–34.
64. John 3:5.
65. 2 Cor 5:15 NLT.
66. Matt 6:20–21; see also Luke 12:32–34.
67. See Luke 9:23; Matt 16:24; Mark 8:34.
68. Rom 7:18–19.
69. Rom 5:8.
70. See Gal 6:14; Rom 6:8.
71. 1 Pet 5:8–9.
72. See 1 Pet 4:12.
73. See 1 Pet 5:10.
74. Matt 4:3–4; see also Luke 4:3–4.
75. Matt 13:15.
76. See John 3:33–36.
77. See Rom 8:5; see also 6:14.
78. 1 Cor 13:13.
79. See John 13:34.

80. John 15:5.
81. See Luke 10:2.
82. Luke 10:8, 10–11.
83. Matt 4:10; see also Luke 4:8.
84. Matt 13:3–9; Mark 4:1–9; Luke 8:4–8.
85. Matt 13:12.
86. John 15:1–2.
87. See John 16:33.
88. Rom 5:3–5.
89. Matt 4:7; see also Luke 4:12.
90. See John 15:4 NLT.
91. 1 John 3:6, 9.
92. Luke 15:8–10.

Chapter 8

93. Eccl 4:9–12.
94. Gen 2:18.
95. John 19:26–27.
96. Prov 16:9.
97. Heb 11:1 KJV.
98. John 6:38–40.
99. See John 13:21–30.
100. Prov 4:23.
101. Matt 16:18.
102. See Acts 4:4.
103. See Rev 1:11.
104. See Rev 3:11; 22:7, 12.
105. Rev 21:5–7.
106. See Acts 9:1.
107. Acts 9:4–6.
108. Acts 9:15.
109. Acts 9:18–20.
110. John 15:12–13.
111. See Matt 9:13; Mark 2:17; Luke 5:32.
112. Matt 26:34; Luke 22:34.
113. Luke 22:60–62; see also Matt 26:74–75; Mark 14:71–72; John 18:15–27.
114. Luke 22:31–32.
115. Matt 1:20–21.
116. Luke 2:7.

117. Matt 19:26; see also Mark 10:27; Luke 18:27.
118. See John 1:46.
119. John 1:51.
120. Mark 1:38.
121. See Mark 6:2–6.
122. Matt 10:8.
123. Matt 10:14; see also Mark 6:11; Luke 9:5.
124. Matt 10:16.
125. Matt 8:26; see also Mark 4:40; Luke 8:25.
126. Matt 5:42.
127. Matt 9:24; see also Mark 5:39; Luke 8:52.
128. 1 Sam 16:7.
129. Matt 26:39; see also Mark 14:36; Luke 22:42.
130. John 5:30.
131. John 8:28–29.
132. Eph 4:22–24.
133. John 10:28.
134. See Mark 4:32.

Chapter 9

135. Luke 22:42–43.
136. Matt 14:13–23.
137. Matt 14:22–23; see also Mark 6:45–46.
138. Matt 6:6.
139. Rom 10:9.
140. Matt 18:20.
141. Ps 55:22.
142. 1 Pet 5:7 NIV.
143. Phil 4:6.
144. See John 10:7, 11, 14, 27–28.
145. Phil 3:13–14.
146. Gal 1:13–16.
147. Rom 8:18.
148. 1 Cor 15:40.
149. Col 3:4.
150. Prov 16:3.
151. Matt 7:7–8; see also Mark 11:24; Luke 11:9.
152. John 3:30, 34.

Chapter 10

153. Matt 15:33–37; see also Mark 8:4–8.
154. Isa 64:8.
155. 1 Cor 10:13.
156. Matt 15:37; see also Mark 8:8.
157. Stallone, Sylvester, dir. *Rocky Balboa*. Beverly Hills, CA: Metro-Goldwyn-Mayer Pictures, 2006.
158. See John 5:30.
159. John 5:41, 44.
160. See Mark 6:2–3.
161. Mark 6:6.
162. See Luke 9:35; Mark 9:7; Matt 17:5.

Chapter 11

163. See Matt 28:20.
164. Luke 23:34.
165. See Matt 10:8.
166. John 13:34–35.
167. John 15:18–19.
168. John 16:1.
169. Matt 6:34.
170. John 13:7.
171. John 13:8.
172. Luke 23:40–43.
173. Rom 3:23–26.
174. John 6:37.
175. 1 Sam 17:8–11.
176. 1 Sam 17:26.
177. 1 Sam 17:37.
178. 1 Sam 17:45.
179. Ps 16:2.
180. Ps 17:8.
181. Matt 27:46; see also Mark 15:34.
182. John 19:28.
183. See John 19:30.
184. See Luke 23:46.
185. See Matt 27:51.
186. Phil 4:11–12.

187. See Rom 8:11 NLT.

Part III: Coaching Others through Jesus' Example

Chapter 12

188. See John 19:26–27.
189. John 13:12–15 NLT.
190. See Rom 12:3.
191. 1 John 2:6.
192. Matt 14:22–32.
193. Matt 14:33.
194. Phil 2:3.
195. Matt 20:26–28; see also Mark 10:43–45.
196. Luke 14:11; see also Matt 23:12.

Chapter 13

197. Matt 5:41–42.
198. Rom 12:11 NIV.
199. Matt 5:40.
200. Matt 5:14–16.
201. John 1:1, 14.

Chapter 14

202. Luke 7:47.
203. Jas 1:19.
204. Luke 6:31; see also Matt 7:12.
205. Matt 18:21–22.
206. Matt 6:14–15; see also Mark 11:25; Luke 6:37.
207. Matt 10:16.
208. 1 Cor 15:33.

Chapter 15

209. Matt 5:8.
210. See Luke 21:33; see also Matt 24:35; Mark 13:31.
211. Matt 25:40.

212. Matt 25:35–36.
213. 2 Pet 1:5–10.
214. Matt 7:24.

Chapter 16

215. See Luke 6:45; Matt 12:34.
216. Prov 17:22.
217 Phil 4:11–12.
218. See Jas 4:8.
219. Isa 58:11 NIV.
220. 1 Pet 2:9–10.
221. Ps 37:4.
222. Rom 10:11.
223. Matt 5:13.

Chapter 17

224. Mark 1:35–39.
225. See Mark 1:44.
226. See Jer 9:23–24.
227. Mark 2:1–5.
228. See Eph 4:23.
229. See Col 3:15 NIV.
230. Isa 40:28–31.
231. See Matt 18:3; Mark 10:15; Luke 18:17.

Made in United States
Orlando, FL
15 September 2023